Stinky Thinking Number 2

ANOTHER BIG BOOK OF GROSS GAMES AND BRAINTEASERS

Alan Katz

Illustrated by Jennifer Kalis

Aladdin Paperbacks • New York London Toronto Sydney

Also by Alan Katz

STINKY THINKING: THE BIG BOOK OF GROSS GAMES AND BRAIN TEASERS
Illustrated by Laurie Keller

TAKE ME OUT OF THE BATHTUB AND OTHER SILLY DILLY SONGS
Illustrated by David Catrow

I'M STILL HERE IN THE BATHTUB: BRAND NEW SILLY DILLY SONGS
Illustrated by David Catrow

ALADDIN PAPERBACKS
An imprint of Simon & Schuster Children's Publishing Division
1230 Avenue of the Americas, New York, NY 10020

Designed by Lisa Vega
The text of this book was set in Aldine721 Bd BT.
Manufactured in the United States of America
First Aladdin Paperbacks edition April 2007
10 9 8 7 6 5 4 3 2 1
Library of Congress Control Number 2006926347
ISBN-13: 978-1-4169-2546-0
ISBN-10: 1-4169-2546-5

To Julia, a wonderful editor who brings out the true stinkiness in an author like me. —A. K.

To Josh and Elliot, my two stinky dudes.
—J. K.

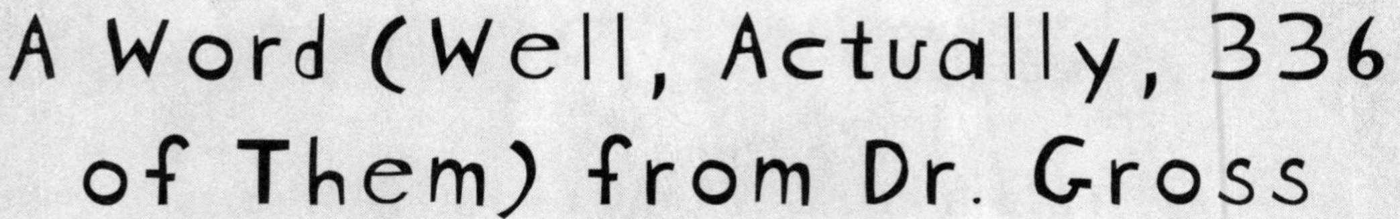

A Word (Well, Actually, 336 of Them) from Dr. Gross

Yo! I am the amazing Dr. Mortimer Gross, the super-duper geniusy-type guy behind the Stinky Thinking learning lab at Hurlbutt Elementary School.

Perhaps you read my first book, *Stinky Thinking*. It was a masterpiece. A magnificent work of literary excellence. A book that millions—yes, millions—read from cover to cover! (And a few of them even read the pages inside, too!)

With hundreds of math and logic problems featuring boogers, farts, poops, dirty diapers, and other very delightfully countable items, reading *Stinky Thinking* was exactly like being in my learning lab, except you didn't have to smell my lunch or recite the Stinky Thinker credo every afternoon. (But just in case you *want* to from now on, here it is: "Stinking is temporary, but thinking lasts a lifetime.")

Simple, huh? We Stinky Thinkers don't believe in complicated thoughts. And we don't believe in repeating ourselves. And we don't believe in repeating ourselves. And we don't believe in repea . . .

Sorry. Anyway, why, you may ask, am I talking about *Stinky Thinking* so much when it's obvious that you're holding a different book in your hands? Frankly I have no idea. It's just that *Stinky Thinking* was a book of such wonderfulness that I want to keep talking about it.

And listen—this book may be even better when it's done. But I'm stuck here in the introduction, and I have no idea how the book is going to turn out. It might be even greater than *Stinky Thinking*, which by the way, was shown to a *New York Times* book reviewer who simply said, "Get that thing away from me."

I'll sign off now, for two reasons. One, I have stinky problems to write. Two, if I do, you have stinky problems to solve. And two, it's not good to write an introduction longer than the actual book.

Best,

Dr. Mortimer Gross

P.S. Did you notice I wrote two things, then listed three—calling both the second and third "two"? I do that a lot. Sorry.

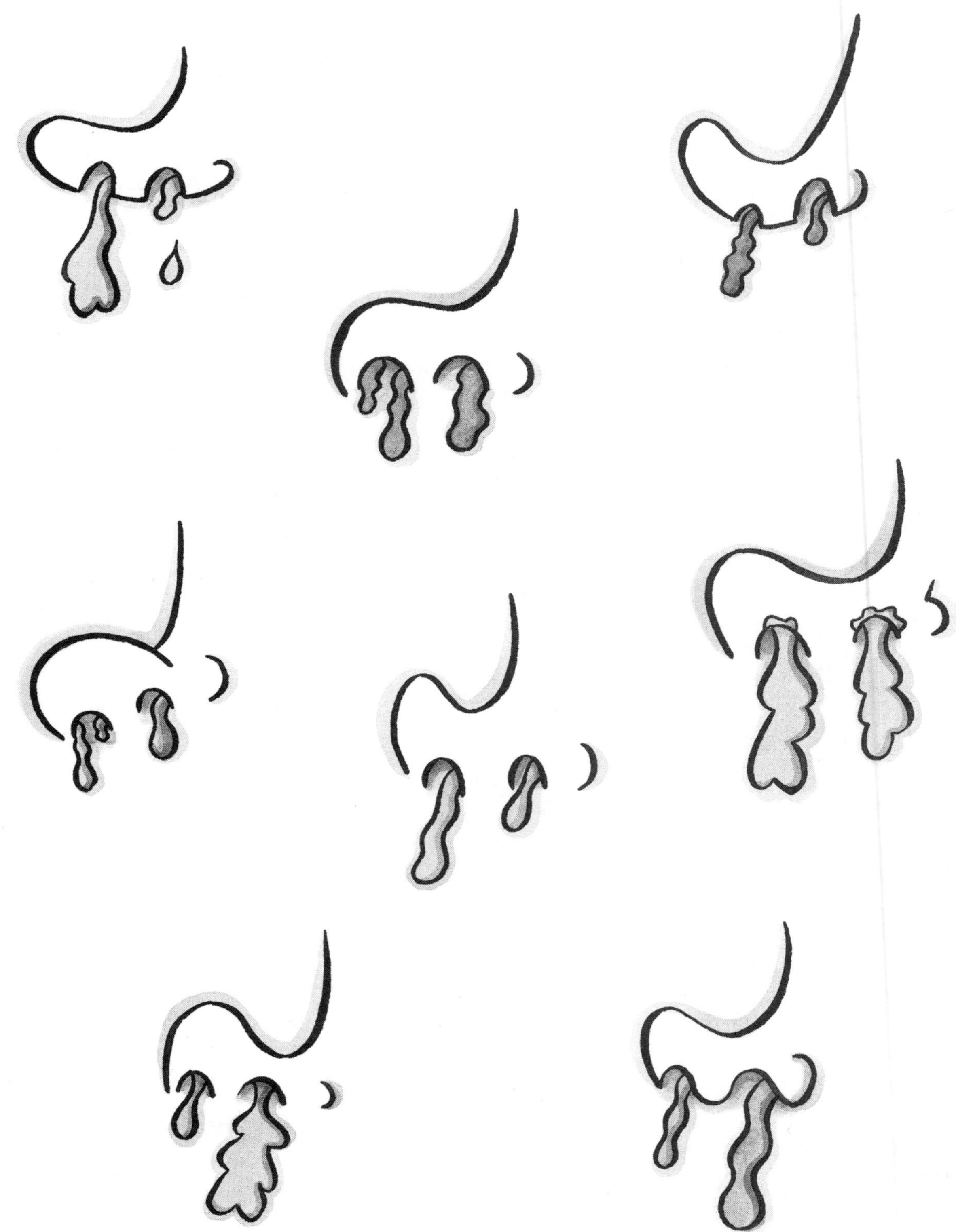

Problem #1

Two of a Kind

Tom's baby brother, Simon, goes to the Terrible Twos Nursery School, and all the tots there have terrible colds. Twins Aaron and Jenna have exactly the same drippy noses. See if you can spot them among their classmates. . . .

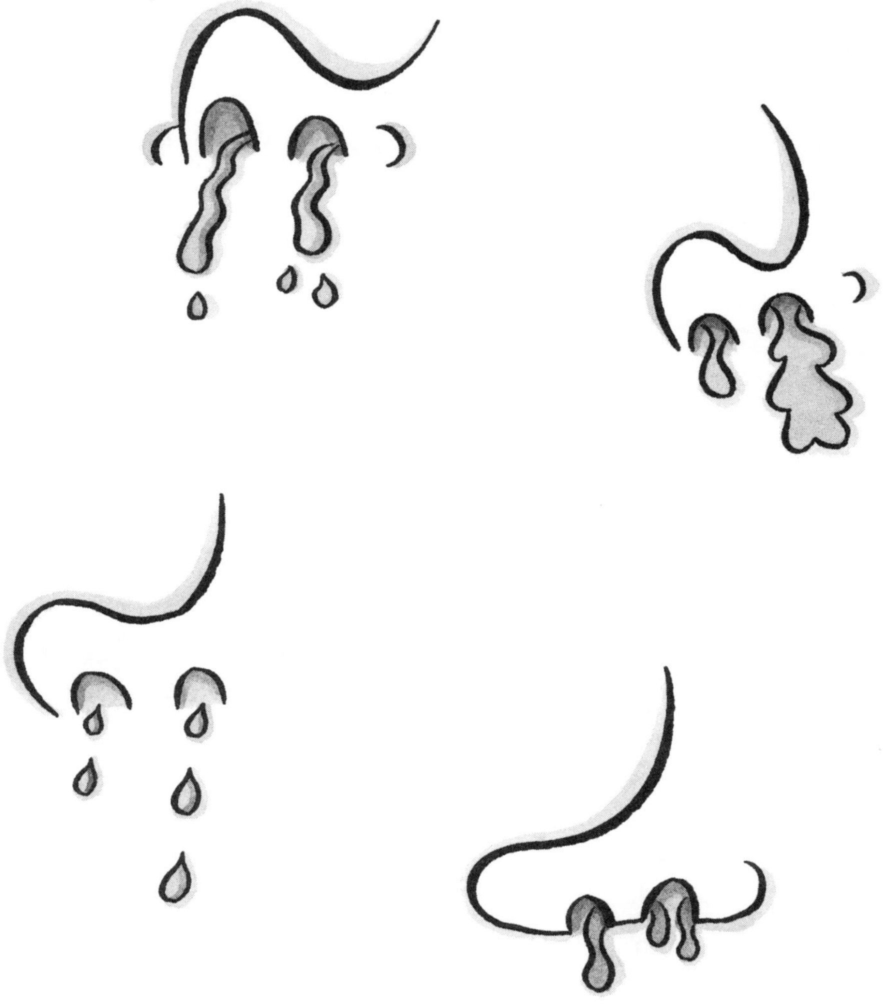

Answers on page 94

Problem #2

This Land Was Chomped by You and Me

Nathan's mom baked twelve fantastic cookie squares for his sister's nursery school bake sale. (They're raising money to buy a new swing set after Fred's father sat on it and broke the whole thing, but that's another story.)

Well, Nathan got home from school and was so hungry, he took a bite of a cookie. Then another cookie. And another. Before long, he'd bitten into every one. Nathan panicked. So he got creative . . . and told his mom that he used the cookies as part of his geography homework.

Take a look . . . Nathan nibbled each cookie into the shape of a U.S. state. See if you can guess the state each cookie represents.

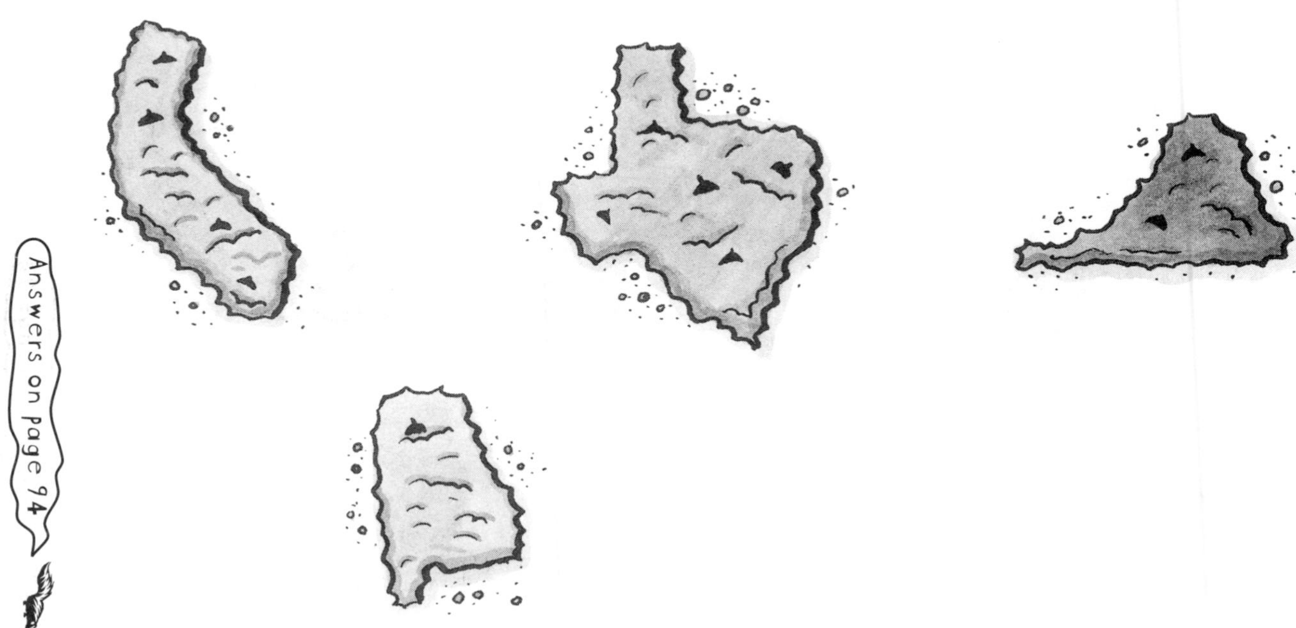

Answers on page 94

Bonus question:

If Nathan's mom made him do ten minutes of yard work for every cookie he ruined, how many hours will he be spending raking leaves and pulling weeds?

Answers on page 94

Problem #3

Find-a-Booger

The word "booger" is only six letters, and yet it means so much. What's more, if you really examine the word, you can find twenty *other* words in it.

Rearrange the letters in "booger" to spell at least ten other words of three letters or more. I'll even get you started with two. . . .

BOOGER

1. BORE
2. EGO
3. ______
4. ______
5. ______
6. ______
7. ______
8. ______
9. ______
10. ______

Answers on page 94

Problem #4

This Is Revolting!

In the country of Toiletzania, they don't hold elections to determine the president, vice president, and so on. Instead they bring the top five candidates to the country's central meeting place, set up five toilets—the kind with the cushy seats—and see who can sit on their toilet the longest. (That's because they figure the other four "don't really know squat.") Anyway, here are the candidates and how they did. . . .

Man #1: 23 days, 11 hours

Man #2: 34,630 minutes

Man #3: 2,095,200 seconds

Man #4: The period of time between April 16 and May 15

Man #5: Four fortnights

Which one sat for the longest number of hours and was named president, and which one sat for the second longest time to become vice president?

Unusually big hint: The best way to figure this out is to convert all the numbers below to hours. (Though you probably knew that already!)

Answers on page 94

Problem #5

Pudding in a Good Word

NEVER eat doody!

On Bring Your Parent to School day, the kids feasted on doody cream pie, which was actually just chocolate pudding with some crust.

After the feast, the parents had to leave. So each kid kissed his or her parent good-bye . . . and there were plenty of kisses between parent and kid.

See if you can match which parent goes with which kid, based on their chocolate-pudding kiss marks.

Answers on page 94

Problem #6

Now THAT'S Really Thumb-thing!

David's baby brother, Asa, constantly sucks his thumb. Well, *almost* constantly. The fact is David has noticed that Asa sucks his left thumb for exactly thirty seconds at a time, nine times an hour. And he sucks his right thumb exactly twenty seconds at a time, eighteen times an hour. Plus, he sucks both thumbs at the same time, once an hour for a minute.

Which brings us to three questions . . .

1. How many minutes per hour does Asa have a thumb (or two) in his mouth?
2. How many minutes per hour does Asa *not* have a thumb (or two) in his mouth?
3. Which thumb looks prunier at the end of an hour from having been sucked on more?

Answers on page 94

Look it up ON the Web!

Problem #7

World-Class Wide Web

Matilda the school's cleaning lady is really, really, really, really nice. But she's also really, really, really, really short and really, really, really, really, *really* lazy.

Being that lazy, Matilda refuses to get a ladder and clean where the walls meet the ceilings in the Stinky Thinking learning lab. And so the spiders at Hurlbutt Elementary School are having a lot of fun running amuck up there. In fact, perhaps inspired by *Charlotte's Web*, they've been leaving messages for me, Dr. Mortimer Gross, and his students. But, of course, since they're Stinky Thinkers too, they've been leaving out some letters to challenge the students.

See if you can guess which letters are missing in each web. After you do, try to rearrange those missing letters into a special message from the very smart spiders.

U___ D E R W E ___ R

D ___ A P E ___

B U T ___

B O O ___ E R

___ L U S H

SPECIAL MESSAGE:

WE ♥

___ ___ ___ ___ ___ ___ ___.

Answers on page 95

Problem #8

WHO WANTS TO BE A DIAPER-AIRE

In *Stinky Thinking*, we played Who Wants to Be a Booger-aire, and the response was so fantastic, the NBS network even offered to make it a daily TV show! They wanted me, Dr. Mortimer Gross, to be the host. Just as I was about to sign the contract, I realized they want to pay me a million a week . . . a million *boogers*! Well, of course, I told them that was unacceptable—I wouldn't work for less than *two million* boogers a week. So, no deal. But that doesn't mean we can't play it here. . . .

But instead of playing for lowly boogers, this time you can win . . . one million dirty diapers!

The first question is worth ten diapers, the second is worth one hundred diapers, and it keeps increasing by 1,000 percent until you play for—da, da, da, da—one million diapers!

Exciting, huh? Then let's stop talking about it and start playing!

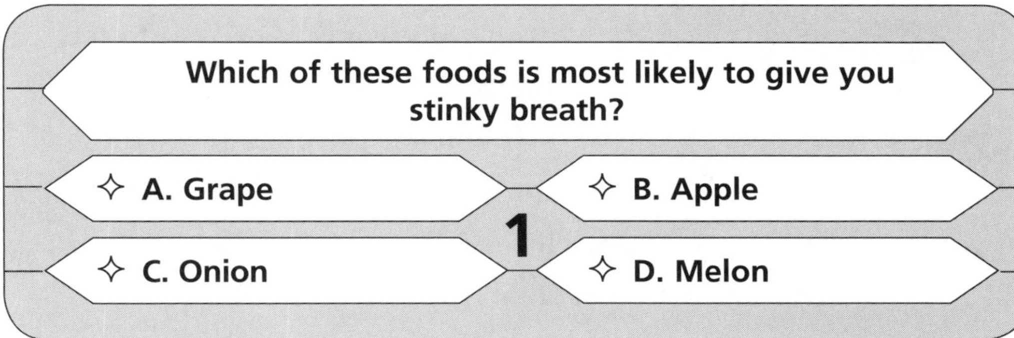

Which of these foods is most likely to give you stinky breath?
A. Grape
B. Apple
1
C. Onion
D. Melon

Answers on page 95

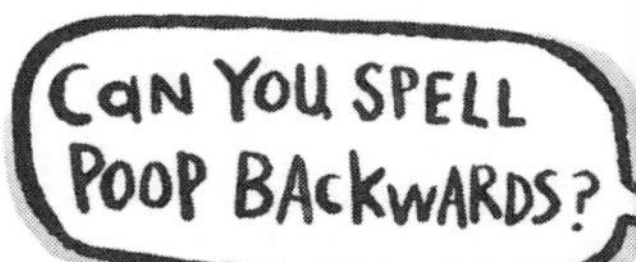

For one hundred diapers . . .

2

Which words, when spelled backward, sound like a lot of poop?

✧ A. Air raid
✧ B. Hot shoe
✧ C. My leg
✧ D. Be nice

Did you get that right? If so, great going. And if not, I'll make believe you did, because here's a one-thousand-diaper question and you paid for the book, so you might as well try it . . .

3

Which of these is polite to say after someone sneezes?

✧ A. "Please shake my hand."
✧ B. "Tennis, anyone?"
✧ C. "I wish for cheese."
✧ D. "Bless you."

The score now stands at one thousand diapers. That's quite a lot of loot for someone your age! Now here's your chance to play on and turn that prize into ten thousand diapers! But remember: If you get the question wrong, you lose the one thousand diapers you've already won, and we'll send them to A. J. Quogmire in Duluth, Minnesota. Why him? Why not?

Answers on page 95

According to official reports, how many toilets were flushed during the Super Bowl XL halftime show?

4

- ✧ A. 10 million
- ✧ B. 15 million
- ✧ C. 60 million
- ✧ D. 90 million

That's an actual fact! And if you got it right, you're up to ten thousand diapers! Now summon up all your concentration as you play for . . . one hundred thousand diapers!

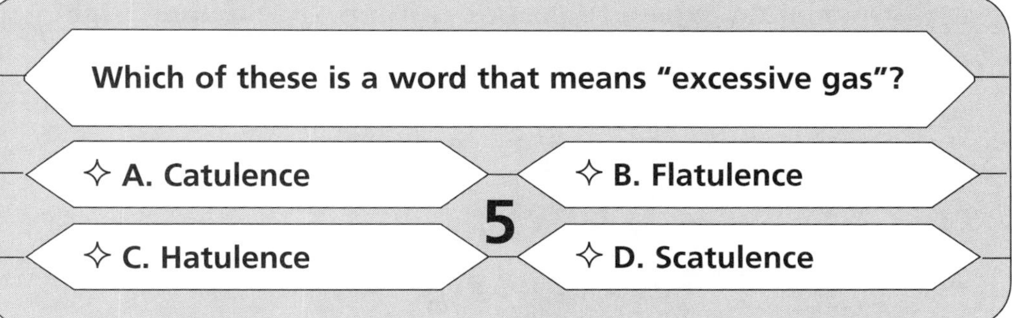

Which of these is a word that means "excessive gas"?
✧ A. Catulence
✧ B. Flatulence
5
✧ C. Hatulence
✧ D. Scatulence

You've got it! (I mean the right answer . . . and hopefully not the flatulence!) Now ask everyone in the room, or the car, or the bank, or the library, or wherever you are, to be silent (unless you're alone, in which case you already know that). Because . . . you're playing for . . . one million diapers!!!! Here is your question:

Answers on page 95

If one hundred babies poop and soil a diaper ten times a day each, how many days will it take them all to poop into and use up one million diapers?

6

✧ A. 100 days

✧ B. 1,000 days

✧ C. 10,000 days

✧ D. 100,000 days

If you got that right, you are the winner of one million diapers! Hooray! But as you can see, it will take the one hundred babies we know one thousand days to poop into one million diapers. Then we have to collect them, pack them, and ship them to you. So . . .

You should expect those one million dirty diapers right around the week of . . .

NEVER!

We're simply not doing it. Sorry.

But be sure to stay tuned for our next great game show, *The Booger Price Is Right!*

Answers on page 95

Problem #9

Phew to Aunt Rue

If Aunt Rue farts twice every quarter hour, and three times at fifty-two minutes past the hour, how many times will she fart between 2:01 p.m. and 3:59 p.m.?

Answers on page 95

Problem #10

The Whole Kit and Capoople

If Jimmy's cat, Sheila, poops on the rug twice a day and Jimmy's baby sister, Lola, does it once a day, how many more times will kitty do it in three weeks?

Answers on page 95

Problem #11

That's No Excoose

When Ricky missed an afternoon in the Stinky Thinking learning lab, Dr. Gross asked him to bring an excuse note from a parent. A few minutes later, Ricky gave him one . . . and based on the ten mistakes in it, Dr. Gross immediately knew Ricky had written it himself.

Take a look and see if you can figure out the ten places Ricky messed up!

Deer Mrs. Gross,
I am sorry my sun Ricky
did not attend your Stinky Thinking
Lerning Lab yesterday. He was home
sick with the flew, and his fever
was over 212 degrees, which we
checked in his mouth with our
best rectal thermometer. He is
back in school now, and will
make up the work he missed,
unless you don't want him too.
Thank yous,
Rickys' mom

A note from Dr. Gross:
<u>NEVER</u> forge an excuse note!

Answers on page 95

Problem #12

The Nosmell Prize

Big news! Dr. Gross is a finalist for the Nosmell Prize for Scientific Achievement.

Here are the other nominees:

F. W. Snodwhistle,
For his achievement in making cars run on dryer lint.

Harold Youwannaslice,
For his work on colds that you can only catch on school days.

Fred Sodacan,
For his work on French fries that speak other languages.

Mel Melmanowskiowitz,
For his work on paint-on gloves and boots.

Please help Dr. Gross win the Nosmell Prize. Find and circle the ten M. G. (Mortimer Gross) symbols on the official ballots . . . and do it now!

Problem #13

JEOPARDOODY!

There's a famous TV game show with a name like this, in which contestants are given an answer and they have to come up with the question. I'm sure you've seen it . . . with lots of smarty-pantsish people winning money by saying stuff like, "Where is France?" and "Who is Albert Einstein?"

Well, this is a brand-new, big-money game, in which all the answers are based on doody. Are you ready to play?

(That's not a money-winning question. I was just asking if you're ready to play. I hope you are.)

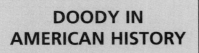

Here goes . . . and remember to give each response in the form of a question, or else. . . . Well, we don't want to scare you, so we won't even say what else.

DOODY IN AMERICAN HISTORY
$100
$200
$300

$100—Since he was the first president to live in the White House, he was likely also the first president to make a doody in the White House.

$200—In the U.S., more than twenty-five million people ride this intercity passenger train system, and many of them make doody in the trains' bathrooms.

$300—It's the number of toilets needed if all the Supreme Court justices had to make doody at the same time.

DOODY IN THE ARTS
$100
$200
$300

$100—Singer of "Oops, I Did It Again," although it's doubtful the song is about making doody.

$200—It's the long-running Broadway show that rhymes with *Doody and the Deast.*

$300—He's a child solver of mysteries whose last name is the color of doody.

SPORTS DOODY
$100
$200
$300

$100—It's the Major League Baseball team that makes doody at Safeco Field during its home games.

$200—Though not filled with doody or citrus fruit, this Florida stadium has been the site of many football championships.

$300—It's the sport where participants need to make a "pit stop" to make a doody.

Answers on page 95

Keep track of your winnings . . . and maybe you'll qualify to play the Double Jeopardoody! round later in the book. Good luck!

Problem #14

Chemical Reaction

The only thing Dr. Gross likes more than the lunch table is his periodic table. That's where he can find abbreviations of all his favorite elements, like Fe for Iron and Zn for Zinc.

To help his Stinky Thinkers remember the elements, Dr. Gross gave the following assignment (see if you can guess along and complete it too)!

Spell the words below by filling in the elements that correspond to the abbreviations. For example:

PICK would be . . .

Phosphorus (P) Iodine (I) Carbon (C) Potassium (K)

See if you can guess the others based on the elements below!

Elements to use (note, all but one is necessary in the below puzzle!):

Nitrogen Selenium Oxygen Phosphorus Iodine
Iridium Fluorine Calcium Sulfur

NEVER play with chemicals!

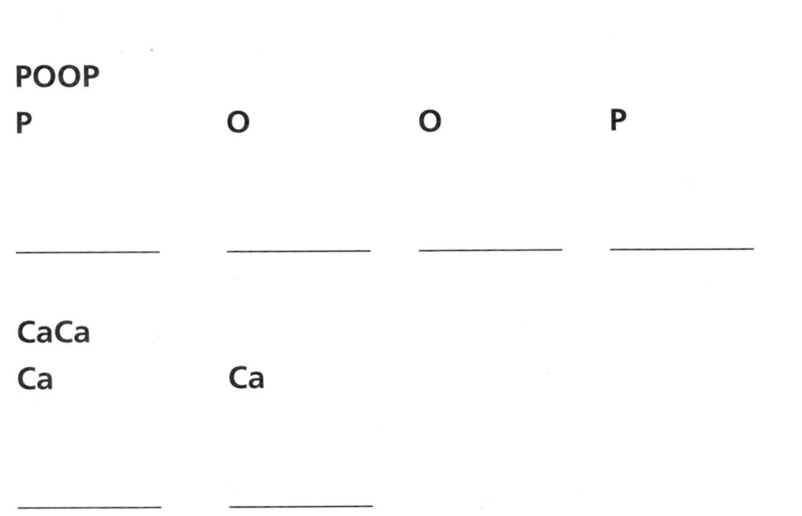

POOP

P O O P

_________ _________ _________ _________

CaCa

Ca Ca

_________ _________

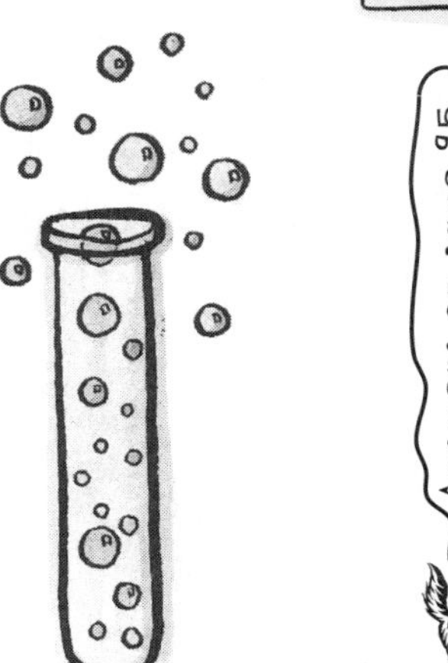

Answers on page 95

NOSe

N **O** **Se**

________ ________ ________

SNIFF

S **N** **I** **F** **F**

________ ________ ________ ________ ________

Answers on page 95

Problem #15

My Word!

Super-Cat actually poops letters of the alphabet! Believe it or not, he poops one vowel (a "vowel" movement—ha, ha!) on Saturdays and one on Sundays. He poops two consonants a day on Mondays, Tuesdays, Wednesdays, Thursdays, and Fridays.

Counting *Y* as a vowel, and assuming he doesn't repeat a letter until he's pooped the whole alphabet . . .

If he poops an *A* on Saturday, March 1st, on which day will he poop his twenty-sixth letter to complete the alphabet?

Answers on page 96

Problem #16

Wiping the Competition

After losing last year's art contest to Tom and his dryer-lint sculpture of Christopher Columbus and the *Niña* and *Pinta* (his family didn't do enough laundry to make the *Santa Maria*), Wendy vowed to come up with an art project that was original both in design and in materials used.

And she did. As you can see, Wendy took first prize for her sculpture of the *Venus de Tissue*. But when Dr. Gross asked her how many tissues she actually used, Wendy didn't know. He gave her five minutes to count . . . and you have even less.

In one minute, count how many tissues went into this beautiful sculpture.

Answers on page 96

Problem #17

America the Buttiful

This summer Dr. Gross intends to drive all around America. And since he's anxious to see as many states as possible, he's devised a crazy route.

Using the map below and the list of states he wants to visit, help Dr. Gross by mapping out his trip for him. (And be glad you don't have to go along!)

Washington, Oregon, Nevada, Arizona, New Mexico, Oklahoma, Kansas, Nebraska, back to Kansas and Oklahoma, then to Arkansas, Mississippi, Alabama, Georgia, South Carolina, North Carolina, Virginia, Maryland Pennsylvania, and

New York.

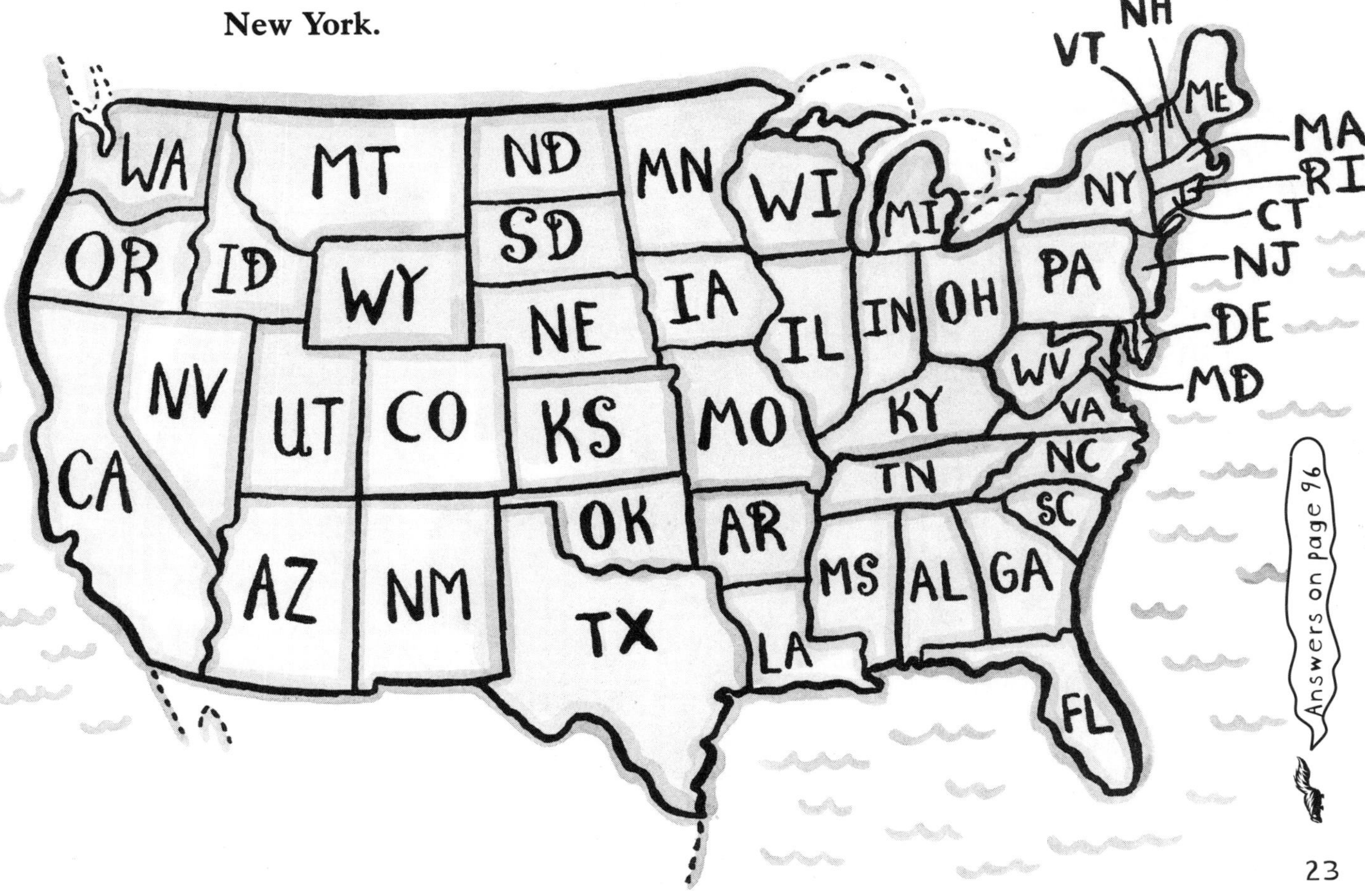

Answers on page 96

Problem #18

Accidental Presidential (Or, Hail to the Hiefc)

Andrew spent all last night cutting out the last names of some of our presidents so he could make a special bulletin board outside the Stinky Thinking learning lab. However, he was so excited to show them to Dr. Gross, he tripped on his way into the classroom, and the cut-out letters went flying.

Fortunately the letters stayed in piles based on the president's last name. But they *did* get rearranged. See if you can help poor fumble-footed Andrew put each president's name in the right order.

HI GNAW SNOT ___ ___ ___ ___ ___ ___ ___ ___ ___ ___

WIENER HOSE ___ ___ ___ ___ ___ ___ ___ ___ ___ ___

LOSER VOTE ___ ___ ___ ___ ___ ___ ___ ___ ___

FAT T ___ ___ ___ ___

IS NOMAD ___ ___ ___ ___ ___ ___ ___

Answers on page 96

Problem #19

A Little Squirt Can't Hurt

Andrew rigged the school's water fountain so it squirts all the way down the hall. If it can squirt two ounces of water per second, and Jimmy's empty backpack can hold a quart of liquid, how many seconds will it take Andrew to fill Jimmy's backpack?

NEVER fill anyone's backpack—or pants—with water!

Answers on page 96

Problem #20

Boxing Lessons

Tom's baby brother, Simon, can pull twelve tissues out of a box in eight seconds (that's because Tom taught him . . . and timed him with a stopwatch!).

Question 1:

How many seconds would it take Simon to empty a whole box of 180 tissues?

Question 2:

If the box costs $1.60 and Tom gets $.40 a week for an allowance, how many weeks will it take for Tom to replace the box of tissues he'd encouraged his brother to ruin?

Answers on page 96

Problem #21

There Oughta Be an Order

Put these scenes in the order in which they took place.

Answers on page 96

Problem #22

It's a Real Pickasso

When Jimmy went to the museum, he saw many paintings that he really liked. In fact, as soon as he got home from the museum, he started painting his own versions of the classics.

Jimmy didn't remember the names of the paintings that inspired him. By checking out his work it's clear he didn't exactly remember what they looked like, either (or else he thought he had ways to improve them!).

Take a look at his paintings, and see if you can guess the true identities of the paintings he was copying.

Answers on page 96

Problem #23

Whee! It's Twenty-three!

The number twenty-three is one of the greatest numbers in the world. Why? I have no idea. Anyway, to celebrate the number twenty-three, try to find and circle the number "23" each of the twenty-three times it appears below.

Why? I have no idea. Just do it.

Answers on page 96

Problem #24

School Play! School Play! (And by the Way, School Play!)

It's time for the annual Hurlbutt Elementary School play, and all the kids are auditioning! This year's production is a musical. It's loosely based on *Fiddler on the Roof*, but it's called *Fiddler on the Floor*, because no one wants to go up on the roof.

The play also has a little Shakespearean dialogue mixed in, as well as some text from an original play Dr. Gross has been working on.

And guess what? You—yes, *you*—can have a part. But . . . you have to read your lines with great acting ability, and you have to memorize them. (You also have to show up for thirty-two straight nights of performances, but we won't worry about that right now.)

Here's the script. Your role is KID FROM SOMEPLACE ELSE. Good luck.

ACT I

Scene 1

NARRATOR: The action takes place in downtown New York City, where Farmer Fred has set up his farm, right in the middle of Times Square.

Answers on page 96

FARMER FRED: Oh my, I am so tired from chasing my chickens all around the big buildings!

POLICEMAN: Farmer Fred, I just found your cow on the subway.

KID FROM SOMEPLACE ELSE [That's you]: Howdy, sir. My family and I are visiting New York—nice goat ya got there.

FARMER FRED: Thank ye.

KID FROM SOMEPLACE ELSE: Farmer Fred, why do you have a farm in the middle of New York City?

FARMER FRED: Because the narrator said that's where we are, that's why.

NARRATOR: It's not my fault.

FARMER FRED: Yes, it is. You should have started with my farm in a farmy area . . . like somewhere in Kansas.

NARRATOR: Okay, let's start over. The action takes place in Kansas, where Farmer Fred has set up his farm.

KID FROM SOMEPLACE ELSE: Hey! I just arrived in New York City!

FARMER FRED: Sorry, kid.

NARRATOR: Yeah, sorry, kid. He made me do it.

KID FROM SOMEPLACE ELSE: Waaaah!

NARRATOR: But if you can do this math problem, I'll change the story and send you back to New York.

KID FROM SOMEPLACE ELSE: A math problem? Why?

NARRATOR: Because I'm the narrator, that's why! Here's your problem: How much is two times two times two times three times two times two?

KID FROM SOMEPLACE ELSE: [You provide the answer]

Note: This play has two possible endings: One, you get the answer right and get sent back to New York and sing:

Oh boy! I got the answer right, and I am back in New York!
Oh joy! I've got an appetite, and I'd like to eat pork!
Oh boy! I'll walk around all night until I find a knife and fork!
Oh joy! I got the answer right, and I am back in New York!

Or, you get the answer wrong, stay in Kansas and sing:

Oh boy, I got the answer wrong, and now I know the score.
Oh boy, I got the answer wrong, it's Kansas evermore.
Oh boy, I got the answer wrong, but please don't think I'm sore.
Oh boy, you see, my family lives here on the farm next door!

So . . . either way, a happy ending! Now take your bows, turn the page, and get back to work!

Problem #25

Wheel of Spit

Use the letters *S*, *P*, *I*, and *T* to complete the names of these state capitals.

Answers on page 96

Problem #26

A Message from Above

Ricky's family car has been attacked by seagulls at the beach! Bombs away! Dozens of birds, and so many poops per bird! And one of the gulls, Myron, is the spokesbird for the group. He poops out messages, and the way to figure out what he's saying to Ricky's family is to connect all his poops (they're the square ones). You didn't know seagulls could send messages? You didn't know they could make square poops? Well, hey, you've never met Myron!

EJF3265

Answer on page 97

Problem #27

Roll Call

If Jimmy writes a letter on every sheet of toilet paper on the roll (starting with the first sheet), then rolls it back up, how many sheets will it take for his dad to read the complete message—"Please raise my allowance"?

Note: Remember to include the sheets Jimmy used to allow spaces between words!

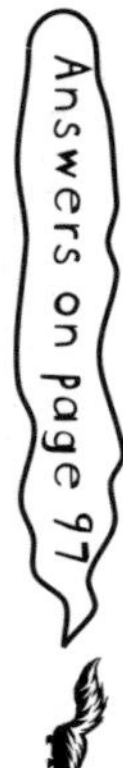

Problem #28

Su-puke-u

Enter the letters *P*, *U*, *K*, or *E* in the blank spaces, so that every horizontal, vertical, and diagonal line has one of each letter in it. (Don't worry about them spelling anything, just make sure there's one of each letter in the line.)

P		U	
	U		P
E			
	K		

Answers on page 97

Problem #29

Brushing Up

Sue's hairbrush hasn't been cleaned since . . . well, since *never*. And she's got so much hair on the brush that Mickey the Ant is stuck in it! (No one told him there's rarely a good meal in a hairbrush.)

Anyway, see if you can help Mickey find his way out.

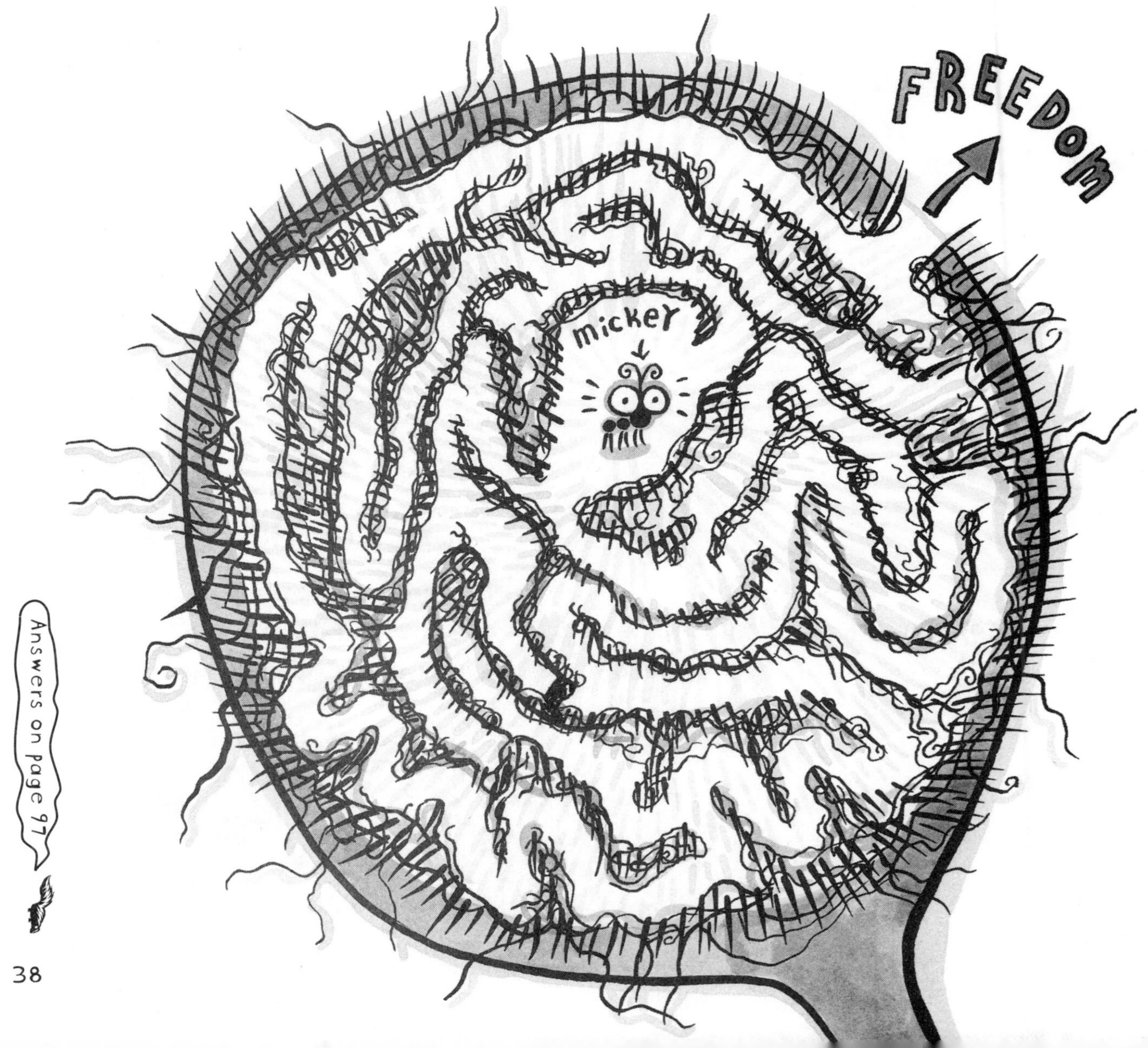

Answers on page 97

Problem #30

Bawling Over Bowling

Ricky couldn't find his bowling ball bag, so he used a pair of his dad's cotton briefs. Ricky then had a great day bowling. He rolled exactly the same score in all three games for a total of 342 points.

Question 1:

What was Ricky's score for each of the three games?

Question 2:

If Ricky's dad makes him replace the underwear (it got ripped, although Ricky's not so sure he was the one that did it), and the underwear costs $6.69 for a three-pack, how much does Ricky owe his dad for a single pair?

Problem #31

Gotta Get a Handle on It

Murray, the janitor at Hurlbutt Elementary, took off all the handles on the toilets of the school to clean and polish. But—oops—he mixed them all up and doesn't quite know which one goes where. Try to help him match the handles to the proper toilets. Murray is up for the Golden Plunger Award from an association called Plumbers of Outstanding Performance (POOP), and we don't want him to lose the honor over some silly handle mix-up!

1.   
2.  
3. 
4. 
5.  
6. 
7.  
8.  
9. 
10. ______

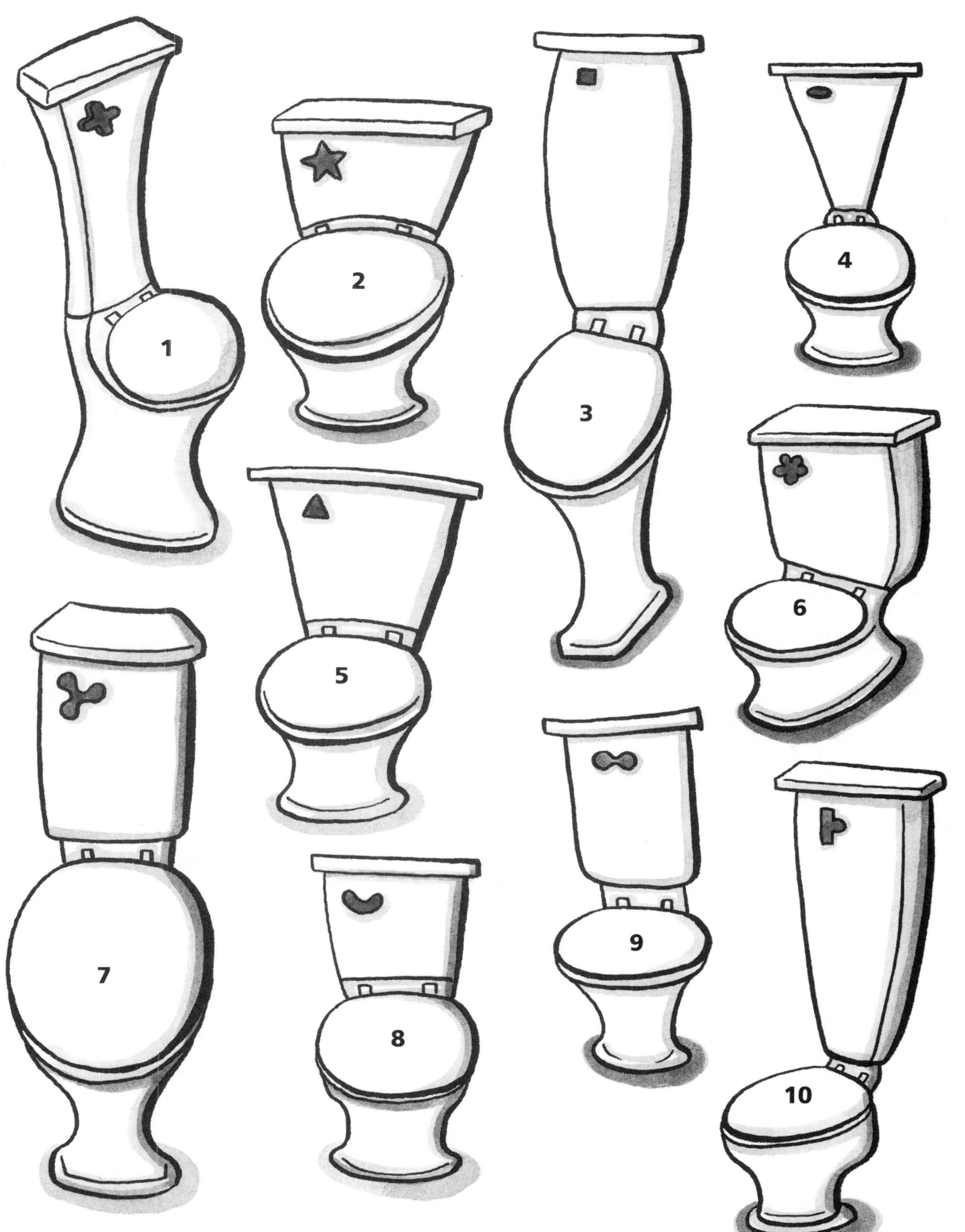
1
2
3
4
5
6
7
8
9
10

WELCOME BACK!

Double Jeopardoody!

Congratulations . . . You've made it! You're in Double Jeopardoody! Again, remember to phrase your responses as questions.

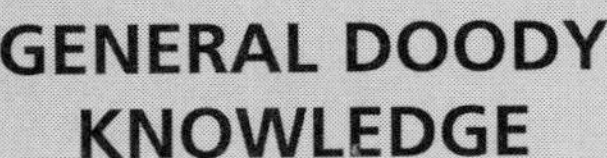

GENERAL DOODY KNOWLEDGE
$200
$400
$600

$200—If all the planets in the solar system were made of doody, this would be the smallest.

$400—It's how many grams a one-kilogram doody weighs.

$600—It's the part of speech the word "doody" represents in the sentence, "I almost stepped in that doody."

FAMOUS DOODY MAKERS
$200
$400
$600

$200—It's the type of animal doody made by the title characters in the movies *Beethoven* and *Air Bud.*

$400—Though his poo isn't a kind of doody, he's the author of the Winnie the Pooh tales.

$600—She's the famous lady who stands with a torch in New York Harbor—and she seemingly never gets a chance to make doody.

Stay tuned . . . Later on you'll get to risk it all on one question in the famous, famous, famous, ultrachallenging final Jeopardoody! round!

Problem #33

Find-a-Toilet

There are more than a dozen words of three or more letters to be made with the letters in the word "toilet."

See if you can get nine or more. Here's a starter . . .

TILT

Answers on page 97

Problem #34

A REAL Smarty Pants!

If Dr. Gross's IQ is four times the length of his pants plus twice the size of his collar, and he wears 34-inch long pants and a 15.5-inch collar, what is his IQ?

Answer on page 97

Problem #35

It All Comes Out in the End

Tom's science project is the study of animal poop. He's got photos of various poops, but had forgotten to label them according to which animal pooped which poop.

Can you help out by doing the matching for him?

Answers on page 98

What's the perfect cure for dandruff?

Problem #36

Let's Shake on It!

Dr. Gross is truly a genius. But when it comes to being tidy, the man has a bit to learn. For example, take a look at the dandruff that's flown off his head onto his desktop. Every time he nods to answer yes, he sprinkles the desktop a little more.

But because he's so smart, even Dr. Gross's dandruff can teach you something. In the image below, he's one head shake away from spelling out a famous quote. Can you tell what it's going to be?

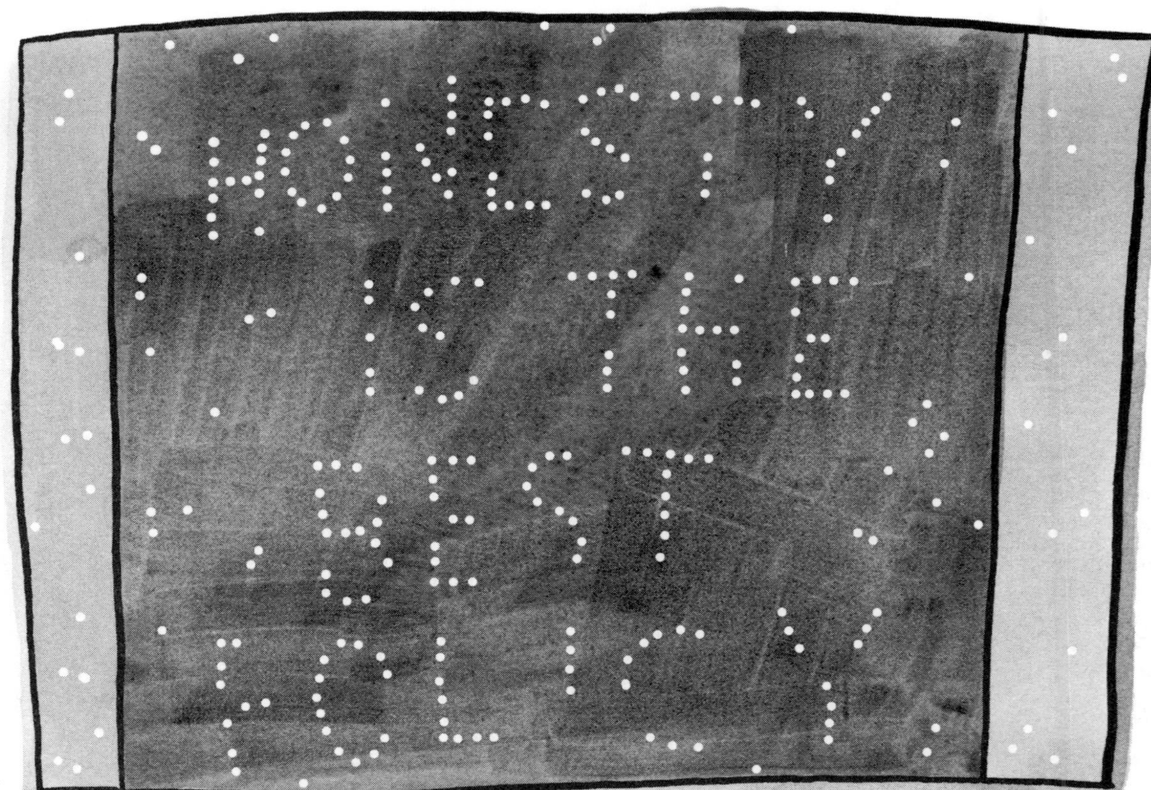

Answer on page 98

Problem #37

To Beach His Own

Andrew and Tom went to the beach last Thursday afternoon. How nice for them . . . until Andrew fell asleep and Tom made a stencil and put it on Andrew's forehead. Of course, the stencil was of a backward word, so that when Andrew woke up, he had a word suntanned onto his forehead.

Based on this backward stencil, what word did Andrew have to parade around school on Friday?

Answer on page 98

Problem #38

Book 'Em!

Great news! The catalog is here from the Smart Farters Book Club!

You can't order any books, but Sue, Nathan and Ricky can. Ha ha!

If Sue orders books *A*, *D*, and *E*, how much does she owe?

If Nathan orders *F* and *H*, how much does he owe?

If Ricky orders *B* and *C*, how much does he owe?

Who spends the most?

Which book did no one order?

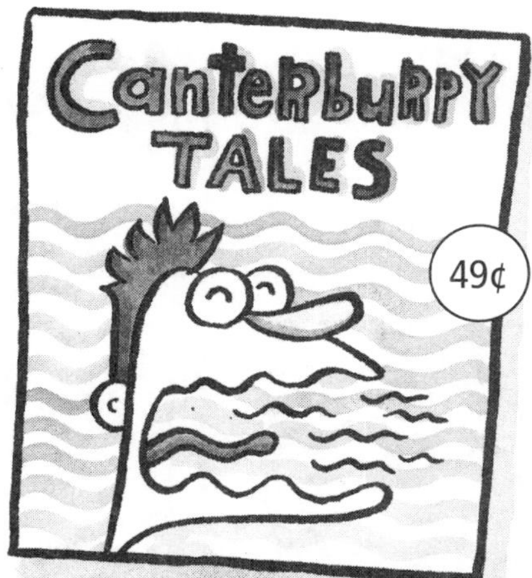
Canterburpy
TALES
49¢

B

AESNOT'S
FABLES
99¢

C

THE EMPEROR'S
STAINED CLOTHES
79¢
uh
oh

D

GRIMY'S
Fairy
TaLES
59¢

E

STiNKY
THiNKiNG
by
ALAN KATZ
89¢

F

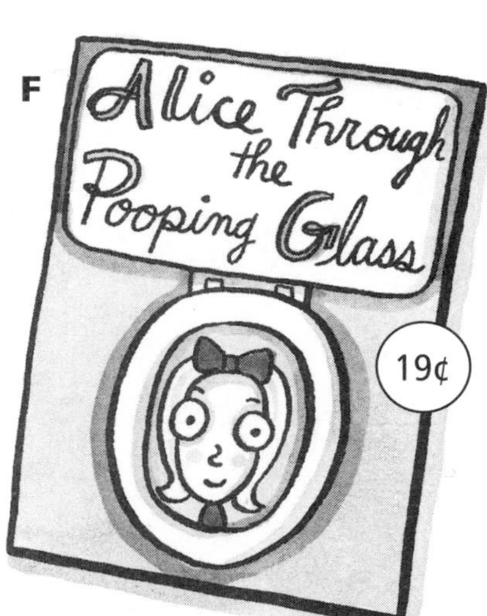
Alice Through
the
Pooping Glass
19¢

G

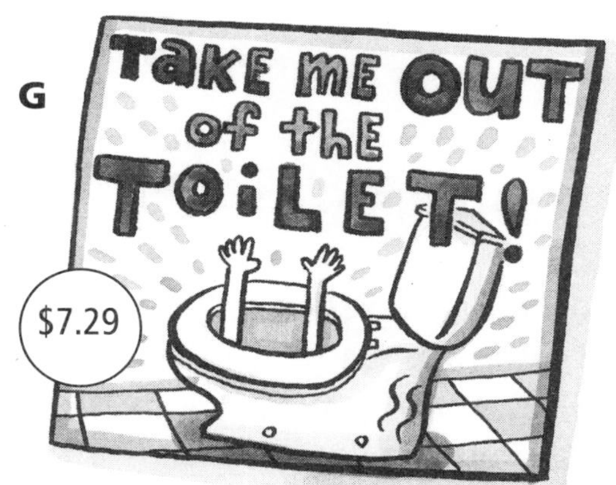
TaKE ME OUT
of the
TOiLET!
$7.29

H

LITTLE
RED
SPITTING
HOOD
69¢

Problem #39

Sticky Thinking

If Tom puts a piece of gum under his desk at the start of every school day that doesn't have a *T* in it, how many pieces are under the desk after forty five-day weeks?

NEVER stick your gum under a desk or a chair. Always wrap it and dispose of it in a respectable receptacle. And if you say you don't know what a receptacle is, that's just garbage! No, really, a receptacle is a garbage pail or can. Okay? Okay!

Problem #40

This One's Rated Pee-Gee!

Read the clues, then place the missing letters where they belong to form the words that all have "pee" in them!

A type of limit	___ P E E ___
It's what you do to a banana	P E E ___
Take a glance	P E E ___
Kind of hammer	___ ___ ___ ___ - P E E ___
Brand of bathing suit	___ P E E ___ ___
A portable dwelling	___ ___ P E E

Answers on page 98

Problem #41

Paper View

Andrew opens a toilet paper stand outside the boys' bathroom. He charges two cents a sheet for one-ply, and three cents a sheet for two-ply. Since there's plenty of toilet paper already in each stall, he doesn't sell much. In fact, he only takes in eleven cents. What two combinations of one-ply and two-ply would earn him the eleven cents?

Answers on page 98

Problem #42

The Gross National Product

Dr. Gross's wallet fell out of his pants, and when Tom checked to see whose it was, he also noticed the good doctor was carrying three one-dollar bills, seventeen two-dollar bills, three fives, a ten, and a picture of himself in front of the Leaning Tower of Pisa.

Question 1:

Because Tom is trustworthy, he returned the wallet with every single dollar in it. How much was there is all?

Question 2:

Which country did Dr. Gross have to visit to take the photo with the Leaning Tower of Pisa?

Answers on page 98

Problem #43

Smartenize Yourself!

Big news from the Institute for Smartenized Brains! Research shows that if you stare at this empty box for 1,441 minutes a day, you'll increase your IQ by 68 points.

Ready? Go!

Hold it! Stop! Whoa! First of all, there are only 1,440 minutes in a day . . . and I stared at the box for that long, and all I got was a giant headache. So go to the next page *now*! Thank you!

Problem #44

Lost and Found (and Lost Again!)

The Hurlbutt Elementary School's lost-and-found room is bursting to the rafters with unclaimed items! Why, there are more than twenty items in this bin alone! Find the twelve that begin with the letters *S*, *N*, *O*, and *T*!

Answers on page 98

Problem #45

Number and Dumber

Here's a problem you might not want to do while eating, so stuff that meatball hero into your pants pocket as you try to solve this:

Total up the amount of even numbers that occur between one and eleven, then total up the amount of odd numbers that occur between twenty and thirty. Add those numbers together, then multiply that by the number of hairs sticking out of Dr. Gross's nose.

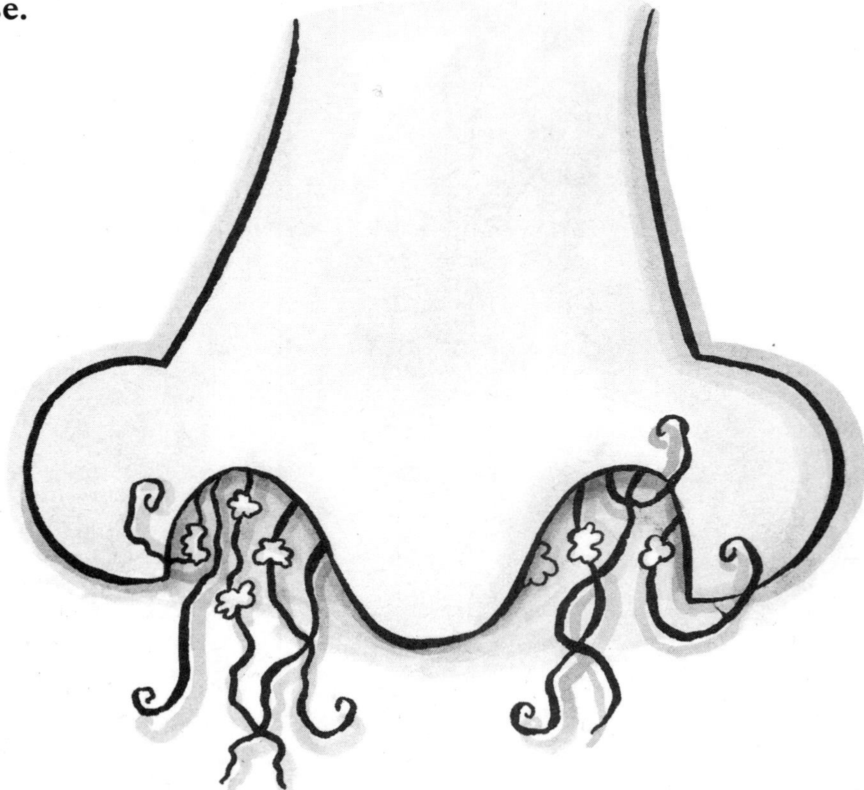

Answers on page 99

Problem #46

Let's Play Farto!

It's the exciting new game that's sweeping the nation! Get five in a row and win! It's fun and easy to play! Figure out each math problem below, then color in the boxes of the ones in which the answer ends with the number 2. When you're done, you'll see one line of five in a row; then you get to yell "FARTO!"

F	A	R	T	O
2 x 2=	3 x 6 =	77 - 5 =	4 x 7 =	5 x 5 =
19 x 3 =	11 x 11 =	9 x 4 - 4 =	9 + 2 =	6 x 6 =
7 x 7 =	12 - 8 - 1 =	FREE	99-3 + 1 =	3 x 3 x 3 =
17 + 5 =	33 - 1 =	44 x 3 =	56 - 5 =	13 x 4 =
24 x 3 =	5 + 1 =	3 x 2 x 7 =	67 - 3 + 8 =	10 x 22 =

Answers on page 99

Problem #47

Field of Schemes

When the kids in the Stinky Thinking learning lab heard that they were going on a field trip, they got all excited. Some whooped. Some hollered. Some even whooped *and* hollered. But here's what Andrew did . . .

He took the parents' permission slips and changed all the names of the restaurants and menu items that Dr. Gross was suggesting for the trip. Can you change them back? *Please?*

PERMISSION SLIP

MY child ________ has permission to participate in the field trip to the following places with Hurlbutt Elementary Stinky Thinking Learning Lab.

BooGER KING ________

McDoody's ________

Taco Smell ________

Fartee's ________

Kentucky Fried Sicken ________

Pizza Butt ________

Bendy's ________

Duminos ________

____
PARENT SIGNATURE

Problem #48

I'm Grad You Asked!

Hurlbutt Elementary School has had some famous graduates. Chances are you've never heard of any of them, but they're famous nonetheless.

Here's some information about one such graduate. After you read it, there are some questions to answer at the bottom of the page so you can prove you really know who's who and what's what.

Selma Schnernippity went to Hurlbutt from September 5, 1978–September 5, 1980, and completed kindergarten through sixth grade in that time. In fact, she was so smart that she went to school one morning and was in first grade, and at recess she was moved into second grade. Then at lunch she was moved into third grade. It was very exciting for her, except that she was upset at missing the first graders' trip to the Museum of Garbage, and the second graders' trip to the Smelltastic Deodorant Factory. (The third graders had already gone on their trip to the Potato Peelers Club.)

Selma is now president of BugDuds, a company that makes shoes and clothes for insects.

Question 1:

How many syllables are there in Selma's last name?

Answer on page 99

Question 2:

How many years did Selma spend at Hurlbutt?

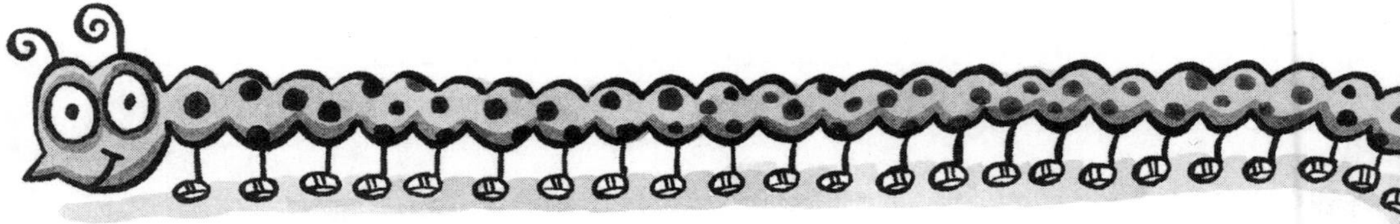

Question 3:

If a centipede has one hundred legs, how many pairs of shoes will Selma get to sell him?

Question 4:

Where did the second graders go without Selma (Don't look! Don't look!)

Answers on page 99

Problem #49

You Look Perfectly Poochy!

They say dogs start to look like their owners after a while. See if you can match these Hurlbutt students to their pups.

Answers on page 99

Problem #50

One Small Step for Kids, One Giant Mess for . . . Never Mind.

Every weekend tons of people walk their dogs in the park across from Hurlbutt Elementary. Many clean up after their pooches, but some don't. So on Monday mornings, the students have to watch their steps as they cross what they affectionately call "Dog Poop Island."

Help Ricky and Sue find a poopless path to school. . . .

Answer on page 100

Problem #51

Algebrahaha

If A x 2 + B = C . . . and B is one poop and A is three poops, what is the value of C?

Answers on page 100

Problem #52

You Don't Say!

Jimmy set the Hurlbutt Elementary record for saying the word "earwax" one hundred times by achieving that amazing feat in thirty-three seconds. Sue owns the Hurlbutt Elementary record for saying "fart" one hundred times in twenty-four seconds.

See if you can break either or both of those records—just be sure you check who's around you when you try!

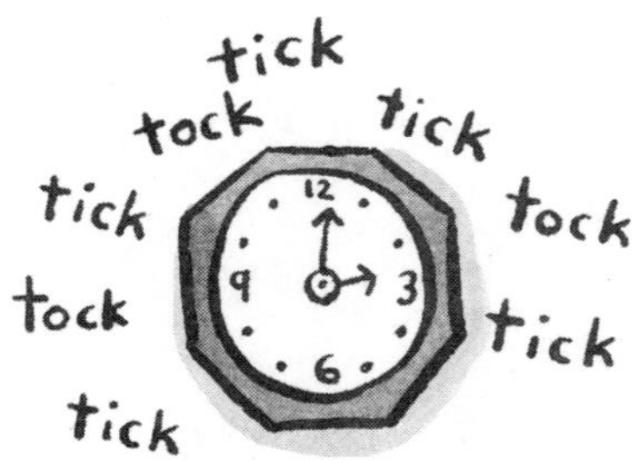

Problem #53

Su-puke-u: Doody Edition

You played it before, now get ready to play it again! But this time, you've got to fit the word "doody" in the blanks.

Enter the letters *D*, *OO*, or *Y* in the blank spaces, so that every horizontal, vertical, and diagonal line has all of the letters in the word "doody" in it. (Remember, the two *O*s in "doody" go in the same box, and two different boxes in each line will have a *D* in them.)

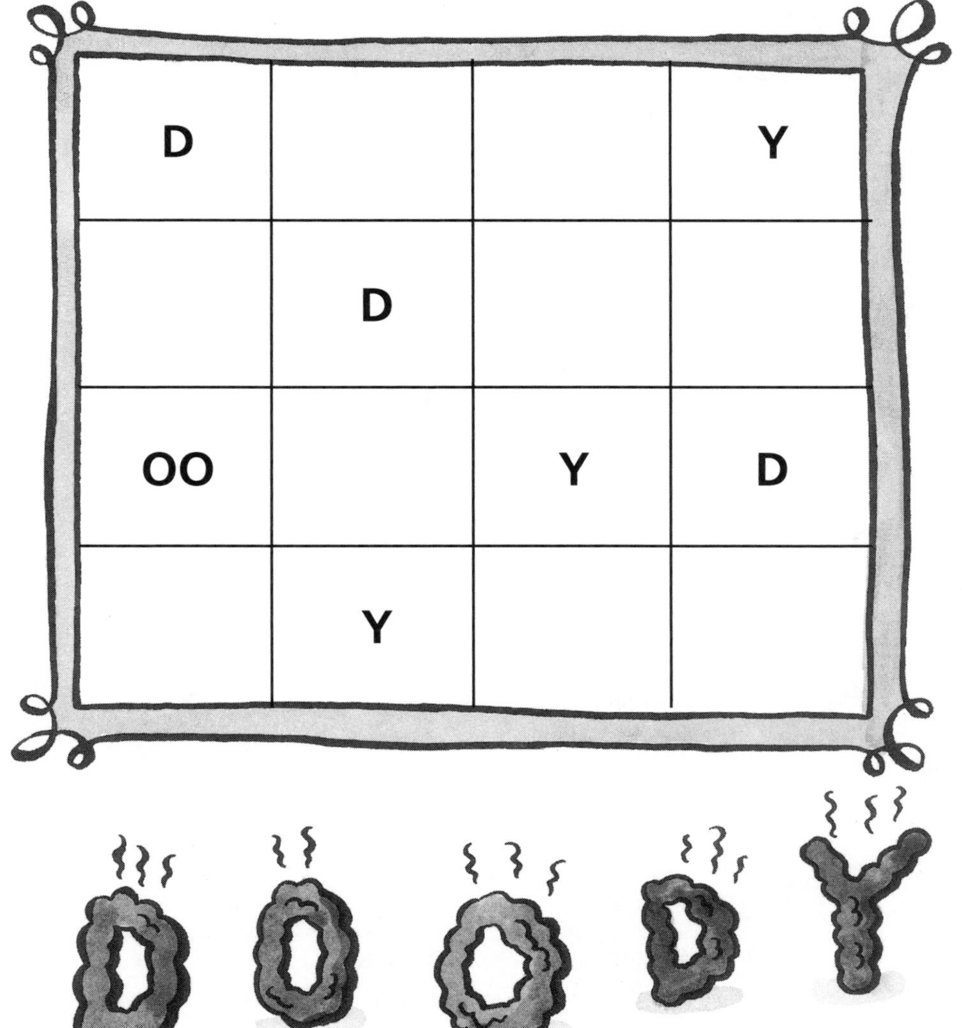

D			Y
	D		
OO		Y	D
	Y		

Answers on page 100

Problem #54

Is Dot a Fact?

Connect the dots to complete a picture of one of the most important figures in the history of education.

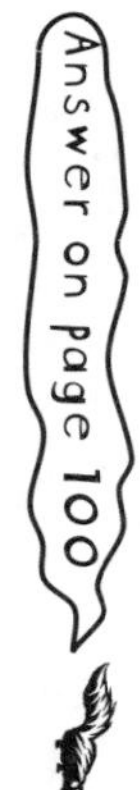
Answer on page 100

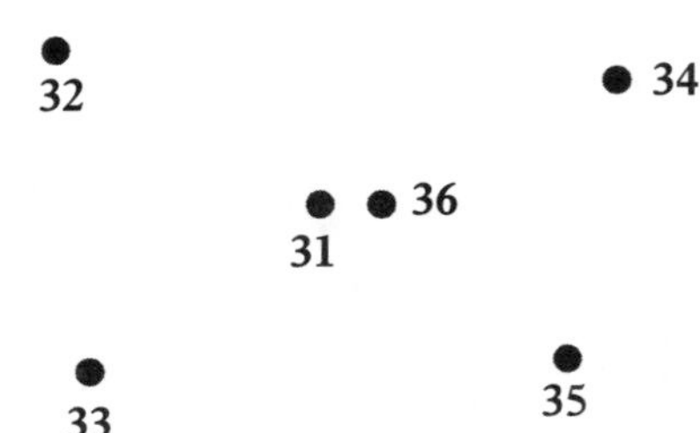

Problem #55

My Fair Doctor

When the kids lined up to test Dr. Gross's new invention, the Grossamatronagasmotelepicton, he had them stand in alphabetical order. So, they stood like this . . .

But when Dr. Gross wanted the kids to test his other new invention, the Shnee, he asked them all to spell their names backward and stand in alphabetical order based on those spellings.

In which order did they stand the second time?

Answers on page 100

1. ____________________

2. ____________________

3. ____________________

4. ____________________

5. ____________________

6. ____________________

7. ____________________

Problem #56

Courting Disaster

If Jimmy could squeeze twenty yards of toothpaste out of his dad's tube of Sparkleshine, how many tubes would he need to trace the outside lines of a paddle tennis court that's twenty feet by forty feet?

This problem is considered for math purposes only. Jimmy would never squirt toothpaste on a paddle tennis court, and neither should you! Now go brush your teeth!
SPARKLESHINE
SPARKLESHINE
SPARKLES
S

Answer on page 100

Problem #57

Picture Imperfect

The kids took pictures of one another for the Stinky Thinking learning lab page in the school yearbook. However, because they were all messing around, none of the pictures are usable. See if you can guess which kids are responsible for taking which bad pictures.

Answers on page 101

Problem #58

Souperstar!

Dr. Gross dropped his cell phone into the chicken gumbo in the school cafeteria. It sunk to the bottom. If there are one hundred and eighty ounces of soup in the bowl, and Rose the lunch lady makes each kid take twelve ounces, how many kids have to get soup before Dr. Gross can take his phone without actually touching the soup?

Bonus question:

How long before his ears stop smelling like chicken after he makes a lot of calls?

Problem #59

Final Jeopardoody!

Wow! Your achievements in the Jeopardoody! and Double Jeopardoody! rounds mean you get to face the Final Jeopardoody! answer!

GEOGRAPHICAL DOODY
DOUBLE
DOUBLE
DOUBLE

You will instantly double everything* you've got if you get this right. . . .

It's a good thing it spouts lava instead of doody, because Mauna Loa in Hawaii is the world's biggest one of these.

***Double your winnings, that is. I don't mean you'll suddenly have two rotten sisters instead of one, or two dirty bedrooms to clean, or whatever. You'll just be doubling your score from earlier in the book. Okay? Thanks.**

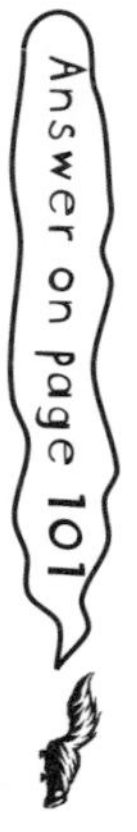

A Message from Dr. Gross

Hello, Dr. Gross here. How have you been doing? I miss our little chats, and I want to make sure that you are enjoying being part of the Stinky Thinking learning lab.

Now is the portion of the book where you get to ask *me* some questions. I have time for five questions, so fire away.

(Ask me your first question now.)

Answer #1: Gee, no one ever asked me that. But the answer is yes.

Answer #2: No.

Answer #3: No.

Answer #4: No. Wait, yes.

Answer #5: $3,234,431.94

Those were excellent questions.

Now get back to work or I might have to change answer #3 to Yes. And we wouldn't want that, would we?

Problem #60

The Sound of Mucus

Tom snuck into the music room and partially erased the titles of the songs for the spring choir performance. How do we know it was him? Because he only erased the letters that make up his two favorite words, "fart" and "snot."

See if you can use those letters to complete the titles . . .

Answers on Page 101

Problem #61

Change, Please!

Change one letter at a time until you change the word "fart" to the word on the bottom. Here's an example . . .

FART
FACT
PACT
PACK
PICK

Now you try it . . .

FART

____ ____ ____ ____

____ ____ ____ ____

____ ____ ____ ____

WIPE

And here's another . . .

FART

____ ____ ____ ____

____ ____ ____ ____

____ ____ ____ ____

____ ____ ____ ____

KISS

Answers on page 101

Problem #62

Can You Ketchup to Him?

Andrew likes writing in ketchup. In fact, he probably has the best ketchup penmanship in school.

If it takes Andrew seven seconds to write a letter, how long will it take him to write (including punctuation) . . .

THESE FRENCH FRIES ARE COLD.

Answer on page 101

Problem #63

There Oughta Be an Order, Part II

You did so well on problem 21! Now here are more scenes to put in the order in which they took place.

Answers on page 101

Problem #64

Just Call Him "Squirt"

Tom's baby brother, Simon, pees in his bed every other night. If he does it on February 1, how many times will he do it during that month?

Note: This problem takes place in a non–Leap Year February (28 days).

Problem #65

With Words Like These, No Wonder He Hid Them!

Just for a joke, Abraham hid the words "snot," "rear," "diaper," "nose," and "fart" in his composition. He did this cleverly, so the words are hidden inside two or more other words. For example, he put "rear" in the work by writing "My friends aRE A Riot."

Got it? Now find the others . . .

A Composition By Abraham

My friends are A Riot. It's not an EXAGGERATION that we tell 100 JOKES a day (though some of them make no sense). I walked far to school, and when I got here I told Randi a perfectly good joke, and she didn't get it. Oh well.

REAR

SNOT

NOSE

DiapER

FART

Answers on page 101

Problem #66

Here's Howie

Howie is one of the learning lab kids, and he was in the first book of Stinky Thinking. He just told Dr. Gross that his feelings are hurt that he hasn't been in this book yet. Of course, Dr. Gross apologized and told him he can have this page to do whatever he wants on it.

So, Howie has asked that you take the time to draw him in the following scenes . . .

Howie as the star of the baseball team.

Howie as the world's fastest racecar driver.

Howie as a champion diver.

Howie as a record-breaking skier.

Listen, we'd never bother you with something like this, but Howie's a pretty nice kid, and nobody wants to hurt his feelings. So start drawing, and thanks.

76

Problem #67

Howie's Back

NO HOWIE!

YOU GOT A PAGE ALREADY!

GET OFF THIS PAGE! NOW!

Sorry, reader.

Problem #68

Not Eggs-actly

It's time to paint Easter eggs, and Wendy doesn't know which six of her dozen eggs are hard-boiled and which are raw. Molly walks in and tells her the best way to check is to smash six. Hopefully Wendy will smash the raw ones, so at least she'll then know which eggs are hard-boiled.

A good fact to know is that a hard-boiled egg will spin on its side, and a raw one won't.

But the girls didn't know that, and Wendy didn't have any better ideas. So she took one egg and decided to smash it.

What are the odds it was a raw egg?

Answer on page 101

Problem #69

Can You Digit?

Andrew isn't good at remembering numbers, but he's really good with words. So when he has a number to remember, he transfers the number into words, then remembers the first letters of each word. Like, if he has to remember 4-8, he thinks of it as "four eight" and abbreviates that to "FE."

It usually works great. But when it came time for Andrew to remember his four-digit locker number, he figured out that it spelled "snot." What's the problem with that?

There are two digits from one through nine that start with *T* and two that start with *S*.

Andrew needs your help. Using his "first letter of the number" formula, please write down the four lockers he should check in order to find his own.

Andrew thanks you.

Answers on Page 101

Problem #70

Crossfart Puzzle

Solve this simple crossword puzzle by placing the letters *F*, *A*, *R*, and *T* wherever they belong.

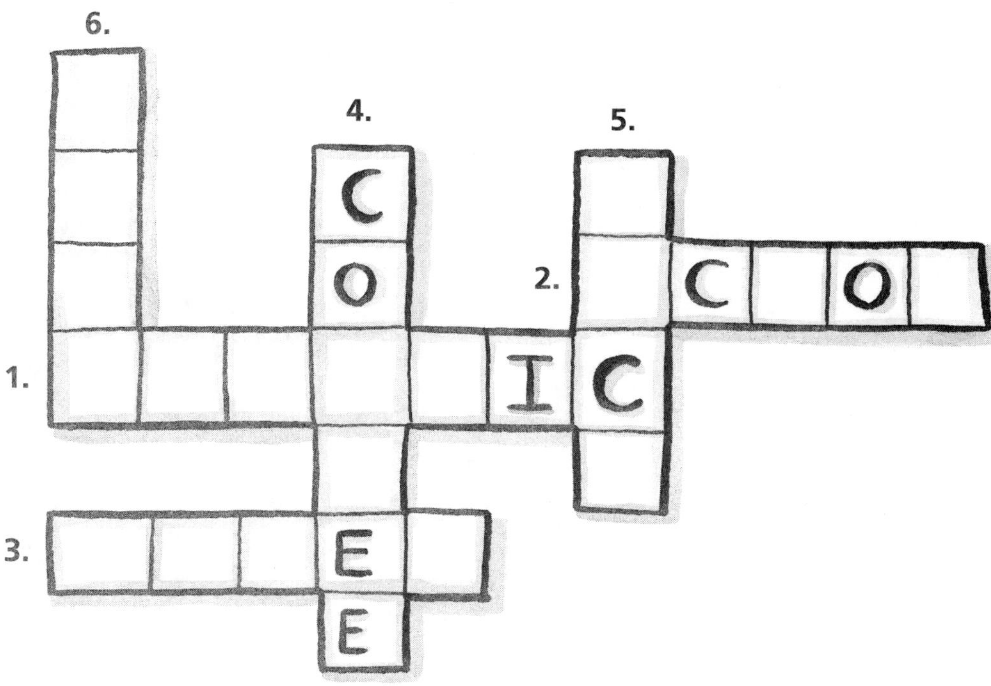

Across

1. Too many cars!
2. Someone in a play
3. Later than before

Down

4. A perk for Dr. Gross
5. Not fiction
6. Go float on it

Answers on page 101

Problem #71

Mr. Break-It

Molly's uncle Sam visits her family, poops a lot all weekend, and keeps forgetting to flush. If the plumber has to come once on Friday, once on Saturday, and twice on Sunday, and he charges fifty dollars on weekdays and sixty dollars on weekends, how much does Molly's family owe for one weekend visit?

Answer on Page 101

Problem #72

I Have a Bad Code

Tom wanted to send Abraham a secret message, and he decided to use a code in which he wrote the letters that come after the ones he really wanted to use. For example:

"ZP" would really be "YO" (*Z* comes after *Y* and *P* comes after *O*).

Now that you know that, try to figure out Tom's superimportant message.

NZ VOEFSXFBS

Answer on page 101

Problem #73

State Your Case

Sue made a poster with the first letters of all the states she'd visited.

U C T C A R K T

Her goal was to get the class to guess which state was which. But before she could, someone in the class rearranged the letters and added a *B* to spell "buttcrack."

Sue was upset, but she would still like you to guess the states she's visited, and here are some hints: She's never been to Kansas, Alabama, Alaska, Arkansas, or California.

Answers on page 102

Official Stinky Thinker's Report Card

I, Dr. Mortimer Gross, am proud to give you your report card to help you show the world how well you've done on this book. Circle the grade you think you deserve.

SMARTIOSITY

A+	A	A-	B+	B	B-	L	M	Q	W	Z

HANDWRITING

A+	A	A-	B+	B	B-	L	M	Q	W	Z

CLEAN FINGERNAILS

A+	A	A-	B+	B	B-	L	M	Q	W	Z

BREATH SMELL

A+	A	A-	B+	B	B-	L	M	Q	W	Z

ARMPIT SMELL

A+	A	A-	B+	B	B-	L	M	Q	W	Z

FOOD ON FACE

A+	A	A-	B+	B	B-	L	M	Q	W	Z

ABILITY TO TELL CHOCOLATE PUDDING FROM DOODY

A+	A	A-	B+	B	B-	L	M	Q	W	Z

Congratulations! You're a genius . . . or at least you think you are! Good work!

The Stinky Thinking Gang

NATHAN
MOLLY
SUE
ABRAHAM
DAVID
HOWIE

SWEATMORE COLLEGE
MATHEMATICS
DORMS
LIBRARY
Shhh
Shhh

A Message from Sweatmore College

Beautiful Sweatmore College, which has been a wonderful institution of higher learning since 1734, boasts the finest students, the finest professors, and the finest classes in the world.

And now that you have completed this book of Stinky Thinking, and you have proven you can add, subtract, divide, and multiply boogers, farts, poops, dirty diapers, soiled tissues, and more . . .

We have a very special request:

PLEASE DON'T COME HERE!

Thank you.

ANSWERS

Problem #1 (p. 1)
Two of a Kind

Problem #2 (p. 2)
This Land Was Chomped by You and Me

 California

 Louisiana

 Texas

 Oklahoma

 Virginia

 Hawaii

 Alabama

 Idaho

 Montana

 Florida

 Maine

 Utah

Bonus Question: 2 hours

Problem #3 (p. 4)
Find-a-Booger
BEG
BOG
BERG
BOO
BOOR
ERGO
GOB
GOER
GOO
GOOBER
GORE
OBOE
OGRE
ORB
ORE
ROB
ROBE
ROE

Problem #4 (p. 5)
This Is Revolting!
Man #5
Man #1=23 days, 11 hours =563 hours.
Man #2=577 hours.
Man #3=582 hours.
Man #4=April 16–May 15 is 28 days; that's 672 hours.
Man #5: A fortnight is 14 days. Four of them would be 56 days, or 1,344 hours. That's a long time on the toilet, and he should be president.

Problem #5 (p. 6)
Pudding in a Good Word

Problem #6 (p. 7)
Now *That's* Really Thumb-thing!
1. 11.5 (30 seconds times 9 = 4.5,

20 seconds times 18 = 6, plus one with both)
2. 11.6
60–11.5= 49.5
3. Right thumb is in for 6 minutes, which is 1.5 minutes more. So it's prunier.

Problem #7 (p. 8)
World-Class Wide Web
UNDERWEAR
DIAPER
BUTT
BOOGER
FLUSH
Special Message:
WE ♥ FARTING.

Problem #8 (p. 9–12)
Who Wants to Be a Diaper-aire
Question 1: C, Onion
Question 2: A, Air raid (it's "diar ria" backward, like "diarrhea")
Question 3: D, "Bless you."
Question 4: D, 90 million
Question 5: B, Flatulence
Question 6: B, 1,000 days

Problem #9 (p. 13)
Phew to Aunt Rue
20 times—twice each at 2:15, 2:30, 2:45, 3:00, 3:15, 3:30, and 3:45 for a total of fourteen times, then three more at 2:52 and at 3:52. That's 20.

Problem #10 (p. 14)
The Whole Kit and Capoople
In twenty-one days, Lola does it twenty-one times. Sheila does it forty-two times. So she does is twenty-one times more.

Problem #11 (p. 15)
That's No Excoose
~~Deer~~ (Dear) ~~Mrs.~~ (Dr.) Gross,
I am sorry my ~~sun~~ (son) Ricky did not attend your Stinky Thinking ~~Lerning~~ (learning) lab yesterday. He was home sick with the ~~flew~~ (flu) and his fever was over ~~212~~ (that's impossible) degrees, which we checked in his mouth with our best ~~rectal~~ (oral) thermometer. He is back in school now, and will make up the work he missed, unless you don't want him ~~too~~ (to).
Thank ~~yous~~, (Thank you),
~~Rickys'~~ (Ricky's) mom

Problem #12 (p. 16)
The Nosmell Prize

Problem #13 (p. 17–18)
Jeopardoody!
Doody in American History
$100—Who is John Adams?
$200—What is Amtrak?
$300—What is nine?
Doody in the Arts
$100—Who is Britney Spears?
$200—What is *Beauty and the Beast*?
$300—Who is Encyclopedia Brown?
Sports Doody
$100—Who are the Seattle Mariners
$200—What is the Orange Bowl?
$300—What is auto racing?

Problem #14 (p. 19–20)
Chemical Reaction
POOP Phosphorus, Oxygen, Oxygen, Phosphorus
CaCa Calcium, Calcium
NOSe Nitrogen, Oxygen, Selenium
SNIFF Sulfur, Nitrogen, Iodine, Fluorine, Fluorine
Not used . . . Iridium (Ir)

Problem #15 (p. 21)
My Word!
March 1–7: Super-Cat poops two vowels and ten consonants
March 8–14: Super-Cat poops two vowels and ten consonants
March 15–16: Super-Cat poops his last two vowels.
The alphabet is complete after sixteen days.

Problem #16 (p. 22)
Wiping the Competition
34

Problem #17 (p. 23)
American the Buttiful

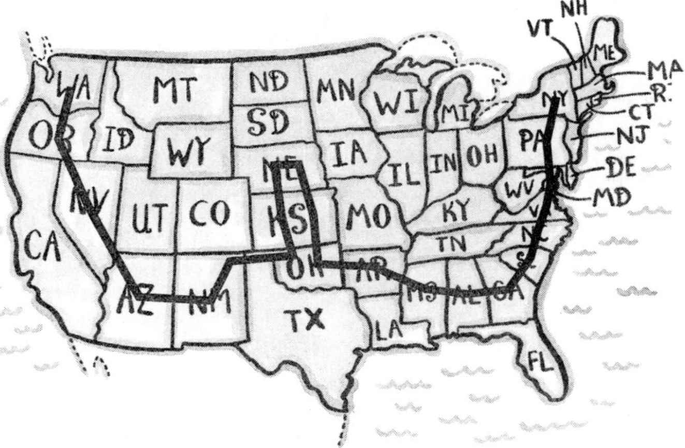

Problem #18 (p. 24)
Accidental Presidential (Or, Hail to the Hiefc)

HI GNAW SNOT	WASHINGTON
WIENER HOSE	EISENHOWER
LOSER VOTE	ROOSEVELT
FAT T	TAFT
IS NOMAD	MADISON

Problem #19 (p. 25)
A Little Squirt Can't Hurt
There are thirty-two ounces in a quart, so if the fountain sprays two ounces a second, it would take sixteen seconds to fill up Jimmy's backpack.

Problem #20 (p. 26)
Boxing Lessons
Question 1: Simon can do twelve tissues in eight seconds, and twelve goes into one hundred eighty fifteen times. So we multiply eight seconds times fifteen and get one hundred twenty seconds.
Question 2: Four weeks at $.40 per week would repay the $1.60 for the tissues.

Problem #21 (p. 27)
There Oughta Be an Order
C, A, D, B
B, D, C, A
D, C, B, A

Problem #22 (p. 28)
It's a Real Pickasso
Clockwise from top: *Whistler's Mother*, *Mona Lisa*, *American Gothic*

Problem #23 (p. 29)
Whee! It's Twenty-three!

Problem #24 (p. 30–33)
School Play! School Play! (And by the Way, School Play!)
2 x 2 x 2 x 3 x 2 x 2=96

Problem #25 (p. 34)
Wheel of Spit
PHOENIX
BOISE
LANSING

SPRINGFIELD
AUSTIN
PIERRE

Problem #26 (p. 35)
A Message from Above
It spells "CLEAN YOUR WINDSHIELD!"

Problem #27 (p. 36)
Roll Call
Twenty-five sheets. There are twenty-two letters in the message, and three blanks in between.

Problem #28 (p. 37)
Su-puke-u
P E U K
K U E P
E P K U
U K P E

Problem #29 (p. 38)
Brushing Up

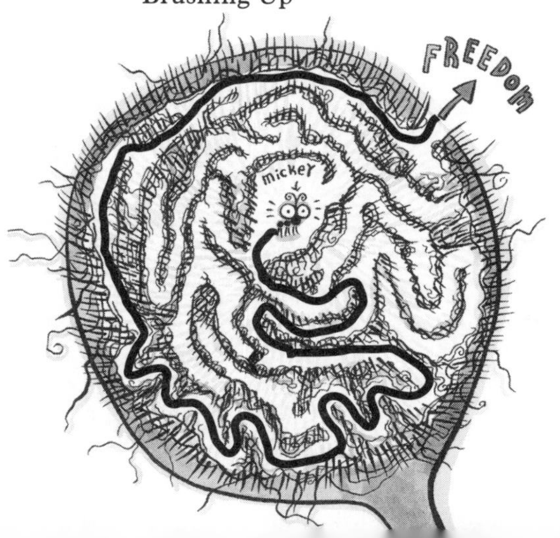

Problem #30 (p. 39)
Bawling Over Bowling
Question 1: 342 divided by 3 = 114 per game
Question 2: $6.69 divided by 3 = $2.23 a pair. What a deal!

Problem #31 (p. 40–41)
Gotta Get a Handle on It
1. J,
2. D,
3. I,
4. G,
5. B,
6. H,
7. A,
8. C,
9. E,
10. F

Problem #32 (p. 42)
Double Jeopardoody!
General Doody Knowledge
$200—What is Pluto?
$400—What is one thousand?
$600—What is a noun?

Famous Doody Makers
$200—What is dog doody?
$400—Who is A. A. Milne?
$600—Who is the Statue of Liberty?

Problem #33 (p. 43)
Find-a-Toilet
TITLE
TOTE
TILE
TOIL
LEI
LET
LIE
LIT
TIE
TOE
OIL
LOT
TOT

Problem #34 (p. 44)
A REAL Smarty Pants!
4 x 34 = 136. Add that to 2 x 15.5 (31), and you get 167.

Problem #35 (p. 45)
It All Comes Out in the End

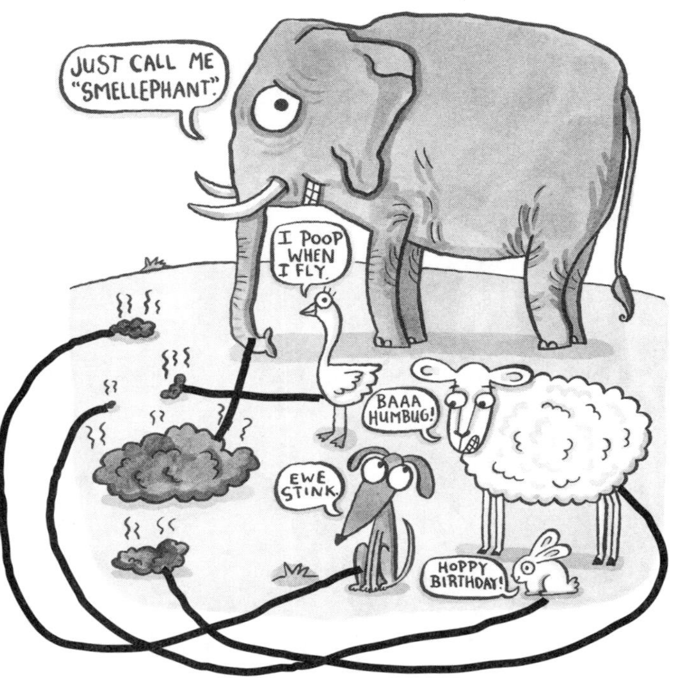

Problem #36 (p. 46)
Let's Shake on It!

Problem #37 (p. 47)
To Beach His Own
GOOFBALL

Problem #38 (p. 48–49)
Book 'Em!

Sue: A, D, and E—\$.49 + \$.59 + \$.89 = \$1.97
Nathan: F and H—\$.19 + \$.69 = \$.88
Ricky: B and C—\$. 99 + \$.79 = \$1.78
Sue spends the most.
And no one orders G., *Take Me Out of the Toilet*.

Problem #39 (p. 50)
Sticky Thinking
Tom only puts gum under his desk on Mondays, Wednesdays, and Fridays (the other school days have "T" in their names). So 40 x 3 = 120 pieces of gum. Yuck!

Problem #40 (p. 51)
This One's Rated Pee-Gee!
SPEED
PEEL
PEEK
BALL PEEN
SPEEDO
TEPEE

Problem #41 (p. 52)
Paper View
One one-ply and three two-ply (\$.02 + \$.09 = \$.11)
Four one-ply and one two-ply (\$.08 + \$.03 = \$.11)

Problem #42 (p. 53)
The Gross National Product
Question 1: \$62
(\$3 + \$34 + \$15 + \$10)
Question 2: Italy

Problem #44 (p. 55)
Lost and Found (and Lost Again!)
S:
sewing machine
snake
soap
sock
sombrero
N:
noodles
O:
ostrich
outhouse
owl

T:
toilet
tricycle
tuba

Problem #47 (p. 58)
Field of Schemes
- Burger King
- McDonald's
- Taco Bell
- Hardee's
- Kentucky Fried Chicken
- Pizza Hut
- Wendy's
- Domino's

Problem #48 (p. 59–60)
I'm Grad You Asked!
- Question 1: Four syllables
- Question 2: Two years
- Question 3: Fifty pairs
- Question 4: The Smelltastic Deodorant Factory

Problem #49 (p. 61)
You Look Perfectly Poochy!

Problem #45 (p. 56)
Number and Dumber

There are five even numbers between one and eleven (2, 4, 6, 8, 10), and five odd numbers between twenty and thirty (21, 23, 25, 27, 29). So, five plus five equals ten, and then multiply that by the number of nose hairs (nine), and you get ninety.

Problem #46 (p. 57)
Let's Play Farto!

F	A	R	T	O
4	18	72	28	25
57	121	32	18	36
49	3	FREE	97	27
22	32	132	51	52
72	6	42	72	220

Problem #50 (p. 62)
One Small Step for Kids, One Giant Mess for . . . Never Mind.

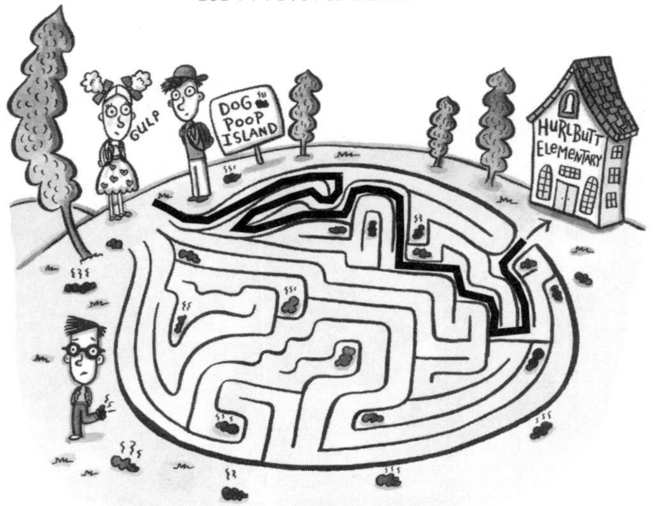

Problem #51 (p. 63)
Algebrahaha

The equation is 3 x 2 +1 = 7.

Problem #53 (p. 65)
Su-puke-u: Doody Edition

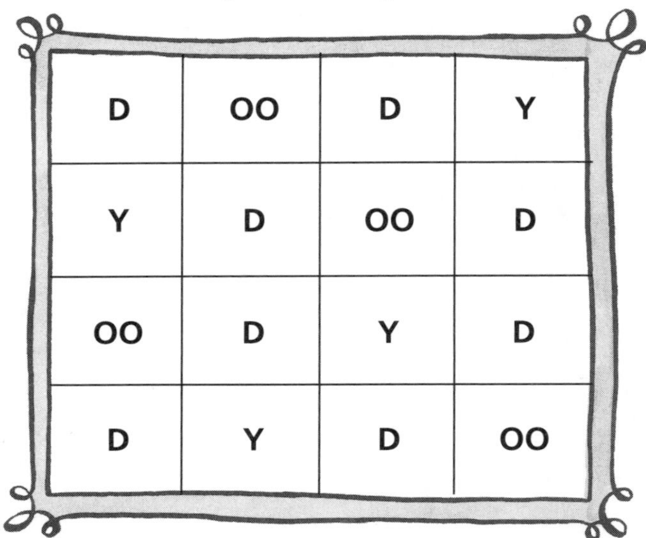

D	OO	D	Y
Y	D	OO	D
OO	D	Y	D
D	Y	D	OO

Problem #54 (p. 66)
Is Dot a Fact?

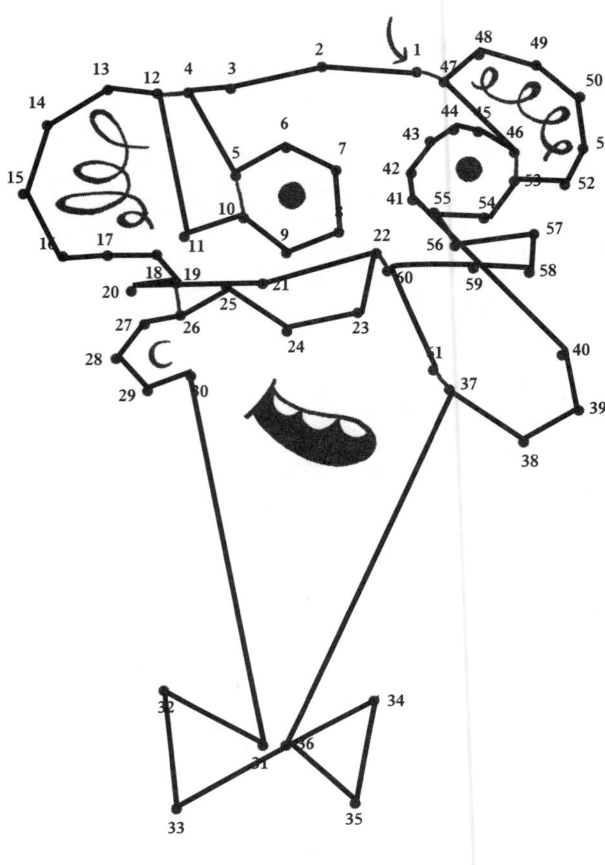

Problem #55 (p. 67–68)
My Fair Doctor

1. BOCAJ (JACOB)
2. DIVAD (DAVID)
3. EUS (SUE)
4. MOT (TOM)
5. NAHTAN (NATHAN)
6. WERDNA (ANDREW)
7. YDNEW (WENDY)

Problem #56 (p. 69)
Courting Disaster

Twenty yards equals sixty feet. A court that's twenty feet by forty feet is a total of one hundred and twenty feet around (2 [sides] x 20 + 2 [sides] x 40). And one hundred and twenty divided by sixty means Jimmy would need two tubes. But he is NOT going to do it!

Problem #57 (p. 70)
Picture Imperfect
1. David took it (he's not in it).
2. Jimmy took it.
3. Sue took it.
4. Andrew took it.

Problem #58 (p. 71)
Souperstar!
One hundred and eighty ounces divided by twelve ounces (per kid) would equal fifteen kids. Yum! Bonus question: No one knows that answer; his ears *still* smell chickeny!

Problem #59 (p. 72)
Final Jeopardoody!
What is a volcano?

Problem #60 (p. 74)
The Sound of Mucus
POP GOES THE WEASEL
FRERE JACQUES
BINGO
THIS OLD MAN

Problem #61 (p. 75)
Change, Please!
F A R T
F A R E
F I R E
W I R E
W I P E

F A R T
F A S T
F I S T
M I S T
M I S S
K I S S

Problem #62 (p. 76)
Can You Ketchup to Him?
7 seconds x 24 = 168 seconds (or, 2 minutes and 8 seconds)

Problem #63 (p. 77)
There Oughta Be an Order, Part II
C, B, D, A
B, D, A, C
D, A, B, C

Problem #64 (p. 78)
Just Call Him "Squirt"
Fourteen times

Problem #65 (p. 79)
With Words Like These, No Wonder He Hid Them!
My friends aRE A Riot. It'S NOT an exaggeration that we tell one hundred jokes a day (though some of them make NO SEnse). I walked FAR To school, and when I got here, I told RanDI A PERfectly good joke, and she didn't get it. Oh well.

Problem #68 (p. 83)
Not Eggs-actly
Six out of twelve—which is half the eggs—were raw. That's 50 percent. So she had a 50 percent chance of finding a raw egg. And she did. Then she cleaned it up and told Molly to go home.

Problem #69 (p. 84)
Can You Digit?
6912
6913
7912
7913

Problem #70 (p. 85)
Crossfart Puzzle
Across:
1. TRAFFIC
2. ACTOR
3. AFTER
Down:
4. COFFEE
5. FACT
6. RAFT

Problem #71 (p. 86)
Mr. Break-It
Friday = $50
Saturday = $60
Sunday = $120 (2 x $60).
$50 + $60 + $120 = $230 the family owes the plumber.

Problem #72 (p. 87)
I Have a Bad Code
MY UNDERWEAR IS ITCHY!

Problem #73 (p. 88)

State Your Case

B

Utah

Texas

Tennessee

Colorado

Rhode Island

Arizona

Connecticut

Kentucky

Notes

Notes

Notes

Notes